A BRAIN INJURY SURVIVOR
HELPS YOU BEAT THE ODDS

PHIL SLOTT
AND MARY SPEARS

Copyright © 2015 by Phil Slott and Mary Spears
Kamuela, Hawaii

ISBN 978-1503107489
ISBN: 1503107485
Library of Congress Control Number: 2014915798
CreateSpace Independent Publishing Platform
North Charleston, South Carolina

CONTENTS

PREFACE

Damage Control assumes you are either a survivor or a caregiver dealing with a traumatic brain injury. I wrote it because I wanted to turn my negative into your positive.

The idea is to speak to you directly and tell you what worked for me. To have a relaxed conversation that gives you hands-on advice about living with a traumatic brain injury (TBI). And, who knows, may even inspire you as you undertake the fight of your life.

TBIs are usually accompanied by serious bodily injuries, but this book focuses on brain injuries because less is known and written about them. Luckily, my creative skills were spared and I've been able to write every word of it during my recovery.

My wife, Mary, has also added some chapters. They are welcome because I don't remember anything about the crash itself. I was in a coma for six weeks, hospitals and rehab facilities for six more months and very confused for two years after I got out.

Mary's notes and memories, during this time, help to tell the more personal and emotional sides of my story. And, of course, this is her story as well. Hey—when it comes to TBIs, you both go down.

One of Mary's chapters tells about our visit to Waimea hospital's physical therapy department in Hawaii. My friend and sensei, Chip Armstrong, came with us because, at that time, he thought I needed it to help me recover. But, as you'll see, that didn't last very long.

Following that, the book goes directly to the problems of living with a TBI because so little is known or written on that subject.

Damage Control not only provides new ways to think about TBI-behavior, it uses a controversial tough-love approach. If this is too tough for you—so be it. But since you're on your own, I thought the sooner you got used to personal responsibility, the sooner you'd become independent.

Experts agree that *Damage Control* is needed because every 15 seconds, someone in the US will experience a TBI. That means there are two million new brain injury victims per year, whether their TBIs have come from car crashes, sports accidents, combat missions or simple falls.

Experts also feel that *Damage Control* is rare, because very few TBI survivors can or want to write about their traumas. Unfortunately, there are many days when you don't want to face your new problems and I don't blame you.

Hopefully, this book will help you accept that condition and the new truths that come with it.

Hey, I wish I'd had this damn thing 22 years ago.

IF...

If you have a partner who was willing to hold your hand at the crash site—count your blessings.

If you have a better half who put a folded blanket under your head and talked to you while you were unconscious—count them again.

If you have a sweetheart who was willing to put up with endless hospital visits, kiss and hug you every day, made sure your IV bottles were full and served as a doctor-cop—count them again.

If you have a lover who carted you around from doctor to doctor or was patient enough put up with your driving experiments—count them again.

If you've got a heroine who fed you, shaved you, massaged you, medicated your sores and pushed your wheelchair around a hospital park—count your blessings again.

If you have a honey who had the brains, strength and work-ethic to inspire you—count them again.

If you have a main squeeze who can deliver the tough love it takes to recover—keep counting.

But if you have a Mary who's helped you come back for 22 years—count your blessings out loud and never let her go.

Chapter 1
Ground Zero

So pal, you've got a brain injury.

Join the club. I've had one since '93.

Boo-hoo for you? Boo-hoo for me?

No way.

Here's the deal: if you don't think about suicide until you finish this book, I'll tell you what worked for me.

Meanwhile, you should know that we're not alone. There are over 1.7 million head injuries in the US every year, including ours.

This whole book was written with a traumatic brain injury (TBI). If I can dig around in my ground zero, you can dig around in yours. It's time we both said goodbye to our boo-hoo's and get on with life.

Whether you were hurt in a crash, combat, sports, or on the job, think of this book as a flip turn at the end of the pool. Now push off and see your next lap as a chance to turn a negative into a positive.

It's been 22 years since a truck hit me and I can tell you, I wish I'd had this book at the time.

Let's get started.

On the morning of October 1, 1993, I was riding my Harley to the gym when a drunk driver sped down a narrow road in the opposite direction. He missed an S curve, skidded into my lane and almost killed me.

The driver and his buddy were dead drunk at 8:30 A.M. I'm sure there were ungodly sound effects at the time, but even if I could spell them, I don't remember them.

My journal said it best.

Do I remember getting hit?
Do I remember lying on the road?
Do I remember my life passing before my eyes?
Do I remember a white light?
Did I leave my body?
Did I see God?
I don't know.

It was a near-fatal crash that left me with broken bones, punctured lungs, damaged organs, extensive blood-loss and a severe traumatic brain injury. Not to mention dislocated knees, a crushed arm and a lot of stitches.

My wife, Mary, drove up to find her bloody husband had been scraped across the road and was lying unconscious under that asshole's truck.

The police were sure I was dead, but the EMS team saved my life, got me in the ambulance and sirened me off to our local emergency room. After that, another ride to Hilo Hospital for emergency surgery followed by a plane ride to ICU at The Queen's Medical Center in Honolulu.

All this waiting time made my brain injury worse than it would have been if the Big Island had the experts and equipment they have in Honolulu.

Over the next three years my anger gave me a booster shot of energy every time I thought about the drunk being arrested at the scene and spending one night in jail. But then he didn't show up at court, the authorities didn't take his passport and he made his escape to Germany, a country with no extradition policy.

Years later, the bastard drank himself to death by developing cirrhosis of the liver.

Hey, what goes around comes around. All I've got left is trashing that scumbag's name: *Siegfried, Siegfried, Siegfried. Fuck you asshole! I'm glad you're dead, you drunken scumbag. The world is a better place without you.*

After the legal maneuvering was done, my brain injury became my full-time job. And it still is.

If you only get this far, remember one thing. Spouses, friends and doctors aside, when your patient days are over, *you're on your own.* I'd like to say I'm there for you, but I'm not.

Get ready to get fierce. You're looking at years of hard work, repetitive daily and weekly schedules, and making the most of very low energy.

In my case, I've been blessed with strong will power, a love of fitness and a combative personality. If your will power is weak, work on it. If you hate exercise, just do it. And if you're not combative by nature, nurture it. *Fast.*

No one else can give you gumption. No one else can get fit for you. And no one else is as mad as you, except me.

It pays to think of your daily activities as two gears. One that puts you in DRIVE, and one that drops you in REVERSE.

Think about it. Having a TBI means after that eating and sleeping, there's no time left to spend backing up.

On top of that, you have dead brain cells.

Dead brain cells!

What's left is a smaller brain to handle all of your basic survival functions as well as daily activities and thoughts.

A smaller brain!

The new you simply doesn't have any leftover energy to waste on meaningless tasks. We'll be discussing how many useful things you can accomplish in your new condition, but it pays to do these things right away:

Accept that you're not going crazy. You've got a strictly anatomical injury. Depression, anxiety, anger and confusion are normal TBI symptoms.

Get used to being tired and assume it will improve.

Get advice you can trust from a TBI veteran.

See a behaviorist to help you understand your new behavior.

Take the right drugs to handle anxiety responses.

Stop bemoaning your fate and start working to get better.

Chapter 2
The Last Day

September 30, 1993
Kamuela, Hawaii

Since my short-term memory is gone, I don't remember at thing about the day before the crash. I only know what Mary has told me.

She tells me we woke up in the first light and saw a foam border framing the rocks up and down the Kona coast. The surf was up and we decided to get wet.

She tells me we hit our favorite surf spot on the Kona coast. She tells me we slid our surfboards under the Bungee cords in the back of our truck and that breakfast was in the cooler. She tells me the first big swell of the season was going to roll in any minute.

Since no surfers were allowed on Ritz Carlton property, we hid from security and snuck through the resort like two scared kids who had get to the ocean. Then, we flopped our boards in the water and paddled out before the hotel staff could catch us.

I would have appreciated that first flop more if...

The air was cold enough for the breeze to give us goose bumps. It was a mellow day and we were the only ones out. Our friend

Vivian joined us and the three of us hooted the morning away, catching little waves.

That evening we had dinner with our pals Leo and Megan who did a nice job cooking and grilling. Mary said it was a fun night full of easy talking, storytelling and lots of loud laughter.

At that point I had no trouble talking and eating at the same time. I was not breaking into fits of hacking. Laughing while eating was not a problem.

I would have appreciated those laughs and swallows at lot more if...

After our night with Megan and Leo, Mary and I drove home under a full moon and crawled into bed. We were too tired to make love.

Now I wish we had.

Mary tells me we were big jocks earlier that week.

Sounds right.

It looked something like this: we surfed twice, ran once and hit the gym every other day. We had two sword-training sessions with our friend and sensei, Chip Armstrong.

Mary tells me that after four years in Hawaii, I was ready to go back to the advertising business. I was excited about a meeting I was going to have Friday night with an old boss who was looking for someone to head up their Asia-Pacific group. I was hoping we could make a deal.

I didn't make it.

Because my long-term memory is still good, I didn't need Mary to tell me that I grew up in New York City, graduated from Dickinson College in Carlisle, Pennsylvania, or that I had a successful career on the creative side of the advertising business.

I remember writing *It's not just a job, it's an adventure* for the US Navy and *Never let 'em see you sweat* for Gillette's Dry Idea.

I would have appreciated my abilities a lot more if...

I remember crossing over to the management side and becoming the Chairman of two Omnicom agencies in the 1980s, in London and Los Angeles. I remember burning out from too much management pressure and having enough money to quit at 49.

I would have appreciated my career more if...

Mary and I met while I was still working in Los Angeles. We moved to Hawaii while we were still courting, built our house while we were still getting to know each other. Siegfried's truck hit me while we were still newlyweds, one year and a day from our anniversary.

Fuck you, scumbag!

I was lucky in those days because so many good things were just normal. Surfing was normal. Socializing was normal. Job offers were normal. Lots of energy was normal. Having a good memory was normal.

But Thursday, September 30, 1993 was the last normal day of my life. After that, it would be a year before I could shower and shave on my own. It would be a year before I could walk up my steep driveway or eat solid food. And I would never surf again.

Never surf again?

It would take years before I could run, ride my bike or swim.

Here are some other things I didn't know. I didn't know I'd be sharing tips on living with a brain injury. I didn't know I'd be speaking to other TBI survivors in language they could understand. I didn't know I'd be able to share something meaningful about recoveries in general. I didn't know I'd be able to turn my negative into someone else's positive by writing this book. I didn't know I'd get more stoked about helping other survivors recover than I was about catching the perfect wave. And hey, I didn't know I'd be able to help other guys stand up and ride.

Chapter 3
The Day

Mary

7:45 A.M., October 1, 1993.

"Call 911. We just hit a guy on a motorcycle!"

Two drunks had just missed an S-turn and slammed into an embankment on the high road to Waimea. Dust was settling around the front end of a pick-up truck when I turned the corner in my car. I slowed.

The first drunk emerged from the truck. He screamed, "Call 911!"

It took me a second to realize they were talking about Phil.

My Phil was under that truck.

In half a second, my heart sank, the blood rushed from my head and I broke into a cold sweat.

That's all it took. Half a second between driving to the gym to finding Phil lying under a dusty truck.

Half second before all hell broke loose.

"You've killed Phil. You've killed my husband!"

Everything sounded like it was coming from a great distance. The bald drunk said, "Him, not me," and nodded toward the driver.

Phil and his motorcycle were lying under the truck. It looked like Phil and the motorcycle had just laid down together in the pine needles.

He was unconscious and having trouble breathing. His legs were bent at weird angles. His red basketball shoes were gone and his socks were bloody. He looked like the wicked witch of the east from the Wizard of Oz.

The driver was under the truck screaming at Phil.

"Breathe, keep breathing. God damn you, breathe! What's his name? Phil, breathe! Don't die on me!"

I was screaming too. "Oh my God, Phil, don't die on me!"

The only sounds were a light breeze rustling the ironwood trees and screams of "please."

The only smells were sour beer, dust, burnt rubber and gasoline.

"Stay calm, stay calm," I told myself. I knew Phil needed an ambulance. What else could be done? All the bandages in my first aid kit were too small.

A couple drove by. They might have called the cops. I didn't know. He was going to die on that road without an ambulance. We lived in Kohala Ranch, less than a mile away. There was a security station there. I went back for help.

"A truck hit Phil! Call 911!" I yelled out the window at the security guard. My tires squealed as I made a U-turn back to the scene.

Every cliché is based on a grain of truth. I learned all the grains that day. Looking back, those clichés were all I had. Thank God for them. They are a useful code; the only expressions that work in a trauma.

Phil's stomach looked like it was pulling air down but his chest wasn't moving. It looked like someone had tried to pull his helmet off.

Phil was lying flat on his back and his pants had bloody spots. His knuckles were skinned, his clothes were torn and his shoes were nowhere to be seen. The driver was still under the truck talking to Phil. He reeked of beer even though it was still early morning.

"Get this guy away from the truck!" I shouted to anyone who would listen. "Drunk, he's drunk! Get him out of there!"

The bald passenger was rolling a lot of beer bottles in a towel and dropping them in the back of the truck. The driver was yelling, "Hold my hand if you want to hold a hand. I hit him."

Cars had stopped on the road. Police were arriving from both directions. Phil was still under the truck.

No ambulance yet.

I paced between Phil and the police car. "Where's the goddamn ambulance?"

One cop held up a bloody shoe. "Is this one of his shoes ma'am? Is he your husband? What happened?"

"There's beer in the truck. He's drunk. Where is the ambulance?"

The driver shouted at the cops, "I did it! Take me in. Arrest me!"

"He did it. Get him away from me!" I shouted at the cops. "Where's the ambulance? Put him in handcuffs! The ambulance, is it coming?"

Some paramedics arrived, an off-duty ambulance team heading home at the end of a shift.

"There's nothing we can do for him without an ambulance. Are you his wife? Which way was he going? Did you see it happen? Who was first on the scene? Where is his other shoe?"

"Can't you do anything for him? Someone please help him!"

"Is he your husband?"

"Where is that ambulance?"

The sound of the ambulance arrived long before the ambulance itself. I remember hearing it and thinking, "Thank God they're here," but they weren't. By the time it finally arrived, I was sick with anxiety.

As they cut his pants off, bloody hunks of flesh that had been held together in his clothes fell into the pine needles. Bones and fat and blood were all I could see. The ambulance crew moved quickly but carefully. Friends and police pulled me away from his body. "Let them take care of him now," someone said.

In the movies, they scrape the body off the pavement, toss the person into the ambulance and race off to the hospital. In real life it takes a long time to evaluate the situation. There are endless blood pressure readings, inserting IVs, timing the pulse and God knows what else. They cut his clothes off, placed him in inflatable pants and put him on the stretcher.

Assessment, assessment and more assessment.

All those things take time. There's total silence. The paramedics don't speak. They focus on Phil. He is the center of attention. They are calm, steady and quiet. From their silence and intensity it is clear that Phil's injuries are very, very serious.

"Here, take this." A paramedic gave me Phil's yellow Casio watch. The stopwatch had triggered on impact. Twenty-four minutes and 22 seconds had gone by. That was all. Not years, not months, not days. Not even a half hour had passed.

Time stood still.

I put the watch on my wrist. I thought, "I'm not taking this yellow watch off until Phil comes home with me." Maybe I saw it was a good luck charm. Maybe it would give me strength and Phil the courage and will to live.

My last thought as I jumped into the front seat of the ambulance was that I could not and would not allow Phil to die.

Chapter 4
What Happened?

Mary

"Phil's been hit by a truck. We're at the emergency room."

I was calling family and friends. I was calling everyone.

Phil doesn't remember anything from those grim hospital days. And I remember too much.

The local emergency room was not equipped to handle Phil's injuries. The only trauma center in the islands is on Oahu, The Queen's Medical Center.

Dr. Elder was the emergency room physician on duty. He told me, "Phil's badly hurt. We can't handle him here. He seems to be bleeding internally, but we can't find it. We want to send him to Queen's, but he's not stable enough—the flight would kill him. As soon as we have him stabilized, we'll send him to Hilo or Kona for surgery."

He went on. "His left lung collapsed. He has a lot of tissue damage. He has had a head trauma. One pupil is responding, the other is not."

The doctor was calm as he said the horrible words. It was like the torture scene in *Reservoir Dogs* where the music is fun and familiar but the action is horrific. *Torture with happy music. Warm, friendly tone with excruciating words.*

There must be a medical school course in "How to Deliver Bad News Without Sounding Like Bad News." Their manner completely belied the severity of the situation. Their body language is one of over-calm, minimal movement. The hands stay down, eyes look somewhere around my feet, the voice is quiet, soft and intimate. It underemphasizes the horrible words being said. It was the only time in my life when a phrase like "the flight would kill him" sounded pleasant.

I kept saying to friends, "Phil's going to be okay. He's extremely strong, he's always taken care of his body. He's always been a one percenter. Phil wouldn't leave now. Life is good, he wouldn't leave me." The pain and fear in their faces disturbed me, yet the confidence I felt in Phil was solid. He would not die.

The drunk driver was escorted into the emergency room in handcuffs for a blood alcohol test. Meanwhile, Phil was leaving pints of blood in the emergency room. Hours passed. Finally a med-tech got off the phone and said, "Hilo will take him."

As Phil was loaded into the ambulance again, one of the ER physicians gently touched my shoulder and said, "He's a really sick puppy. Go touch him. Talk to him. Tell him you're here." But I didn't know where to touch him exactly, so I leaned over and kissed his forehead and said, "Phil, I love you. Don't leave me now."

My last glimpse of home for months was from the front seat of an ambulance, looking back into faces of worried friends.

If I had a gun, I would have been shooting cars left and right on that ride to Hilo. The Hamakua coast is a beautiful and challenging road to drive when life is fine. When life is not so fine, it is tortuous. The winding, narrow road was slow because of sleepy commuters going 25 miles per hour. There is no safe way to get around them—no shoulders, no passing zones. Even though the siren was screaming, cars just ignored us. The ambulance was six feet from the car in front of us. The siren was wailing and the lights were flashing, but they kept acting like we weren't even there.

I kept checking on Phil in the back. Charlie Whittle, the paramedic, and a nurse from the medical center were busily working on him, checking and re-checking.

There were more sleepy drivers on the road. It was all I could do not to swear out the window. Check on Phil. Scan the road. Check on Phil. As if by looking out for slow cars, I could will them out of the way.

As we arrived in Hilo, the back of the ambulance became quiet. Charlie and the nurse were no longer moving around. They sat quietly by Phil's side. Charlie looked at me with the saddest eyes I've ever seen and smiled apologetically. I was sick with fear.

But the angels were with us. We pulled into the Hilo Hospital emergency room and Phil went straight from the ambulance to the operating room. The operating room was prepped for someone else but they just slipped Phil in first. *Thank you.* Whoever was scheduled for that operating room table, thank you. Without that lucky break, Phil would be dead today.

Waiting rooms in hospitals are the same anywhere. Uncomfortable chairs arranged in a corner, lots of linoleum, pale pastel colors, mostly bare walls and bad fluorescent lighting. After all the panic and noise, I was surrounded by the silence and solitude.

Alone. Cold. Wearing gym shorts, a T-shirt, tennis shoes. I had my purse, credit cards and cash. Our friend Mike arrived with phone numbers and a bag of clothes for Oahu. I started making the calls.

My parents: "Phil has been hit by a truck. No, don't come yet. Let me see what the situation is."

Phil's brother: "Phil's been hit by a truck. Will you call your parents? It's really bad."

After several hours, I was allowed into the recovery room. He looked worse, his body extremely swollen and discolored. His left leg was in some kind of inflatable splint, a dark, dark blue. His right leg was four times its normal size. Bandages, oxygen, bruising—it was the first time I'd done an inventory of his body. It didn't look good.

I started talking to him. Talking and whispering that it would be okay. Telling him what happened. Telling him about his injuries. About how much I loved him. I stroked the only unbandaged spot on his right thigh, telling him life was good.

How much did I weigh? Could I ride with Phil on the medevac airplane? Was he stable enough? Did they get authorization from Queen's? Was the airplane available? Phone calls back and forth.

Finally, go.

Then, hurry up and wait. Everything was painstakingly slow. Prepping him for the ambulance. Loading and unloading Phil from a gurney at the hospital took almost an hour.

Ambulance to the airport. Through the back gate. Past the trucks full of workers drinking cases of beer. Where were the police? These dangerous, stupid, hateful drunks were just waiting until they were so drunk they couldn't see to get in their trucks and drive home and maybe kill themselves, but more likely kill someone else. I hated them. I wanted to go slash their tires and scream.

"Tie him on the stretcher."

The air ambulance was a very small plane. Propeller driven. It wasn't clear how we'd get Phil through the doorway. He was lying on a long, wide stretcher.

Unload, check vital signs, reload, more vital signs. How to get him in? The ambulance crew, the pilot and I held onto the stretcher. We lifted, angled. Phil was strapped down like a crate on a palette. We turned him sideways and slid him in.

The harvest moon was rising, the sun was setting, and ours was the only airplane moving at Hilo International Airport. We flew low in the sky. Mauna Kea towered above us. The plane was so low that all the details below were clear in the soft pink light of a tropical sunset. The flight took us in and out of clouds, rain, turbulence and past Maui's Haleakala on our right. Phil was in the back with two paramedics who kept moving through the litany of vital signs. I was in the co-pilot's seat. The world around me was spectacular. The experience was surreal.

A heavy, dull flatness sat on me as hours of fear and anxiety settled into my stomach. A perfect tropical sunset preceded the darkness.

Queen's hospital at last. The state's trauma center, the Hawaiian Mecca of health care. Phil was whisked into surgery before I could touch him again.

I walked into the caring arms of friends. The paperwork was handled, the physicians were ready and my overnight bag was waiting. Our friends were sitting on a bench in the emergency room waiting for us to arrive.

Lots of anxious sitting and anxious talking. Hours went by. Phil was in surgery, the rest of us sitting in the Intensive Care waiting room.

A flurry of surgeons came in.

"We may have to take the leg from the knee."

No way, I thought.

"Or take the foot."

Definitely not.

"Or take the heel or some portion of it."

Let's focus on saving, not removing!

The orthopedic surgeon continued to explain the state of his left leg. "It looks like he's been flayed. We don't know whether or not the leg will make it. The tissue damage is more severe going down the leg. At this point in time, we don't know. We'll have to give it a few days."

"No way to know," the trauma surgeon repeated. "He's had a severe trauma to his abdomen. Lots of bruising of the internal organs. We'll have to wait and see what the situation is."

"He's had brain damage," the neurosurgeon said. "He has a subdural hematoma on the right side of his head between the frontal lobe and the cerebellum. The CAT scan indicates that he has some pinprick bleeding between the brain hemispheres near the brain stem and cerebellum. We won't know about any permanent damage for a while."

"We'll have to wait and see what happens. We'll have to go in again later, after a few days and do some muscle and skin grafting to cover the holes," the plastic surgeon said.

Then they all started interrupting each other.

"The body is a miraculous thing…"

"We cleaned everything out to make sure no infection develops…"

"We'll go back in and fix him up…"

"I've seen heels and legs that looked much worse than that, Phil's will heal nicely…"

"Give it time…"

"It's too early to tell, but I believe that everything just might turn out all right…"

"He handled the surgery well…"

"Just hang in there…"

And on it went.

I only had two questions. "Is Phil going to live? Is he going to recover?" That was all I wanted to know.

No one except God could tell me. The doctors could only tell me what they knew right now. I heard, but didn't understand.

The one thing I did understand was amputation. I did get that one. And I did understand hope and promise. "The human body is miraculous." I understood that, so that's what I hung on to.

Big Brother cameras. Industrial gray walls. Hard concrete floors. The smell of acrid cleaners and oxygen. People dressed in green and white. Androgynous uniforms bustling around the body. ICU is an alien world.

After 2:00 A.M. I was finally able to touch Phil, to make sure he was alive. The ER room was extremely cold with lots of bright flickering fluorescent lights, beepers for each heart beat, gasping machines, sirens, alarms.

Tubes in every opening. The one in his nose that looked much larger than the one in his throat. Bags of urine hung from the sides of the bed. Incision lines and staples covered his gut. Cuts, scrapes and miscellaneous holes were open to the air. Bandages covered the extreme tissue damage. His flesh was bruised black, green and purple. His hair was matted with dirt and pine needles. He was naked except for a small, white hand towel.

Where could I touch him? I was intimidated.

The only clear places visible were his right temple, the big toe on his right foot and the pinkie finger on his right hand. I touched all three places and leaned over a machine to kiss his head. A nurse gave me some of Phil's hair that used to be on his head.

"How maudlin," I said to myself, then stuffed the hair in a plastic bag. A treasure that has never left me.

"Pizza, sandwiches, something to drink?"

"Eat, you must eat, you'll never make it through this if you don't eat."

Thank God for friends. They think of things like food and sleep.

We settled in for the night at the Queen's ICU waiting room. We lay on the floor under blankets from the operating room. I used a book bag for a pillow. I moved from the bench to the floor and back again looking for a place to get settled. I watched the security guards going by.

Would Phil ever come home? Would Phil ever be Phil again? Was this the end? Would I ever sleep again? Months would go by before I could do anything more than get through the night.

Finally, the night was over.

Chapter 5
The New Me Stinks

Every business stresses the word new for a good reason. Americans are obsessed with new-ness of all kinds. From new and improved laundry products and kitchen conveniences, to brand-new destination resorts and the cruise ships that get them there. We just can't help believing that new ships, new cars, new houses, new recipes, new clothes, new gadgets and even new colognes will make a huge improvement in our daily lives.

But new doesn't always mean better. No, pal, this time the new me is a worse me. I didn't remember when the new me woke up from a six week coma at Queen's hospital. I was so groggy that I didn't understand what had happened to me. I was confused, dizzy and unable to speak.

My first memories are strangely objective. Like a medical student observing a patient with a unique condition. In fact, it took months before I realized this new me really *was* me.

Then, after months of semi-consciousness, exhaustion, IV dripping and dial checking, I realized that everything stunk for the first time in my life.

If everything stinks for the first time in your life too, hang in there, you just need to face some new facts.

Even though you have many of the same symptoms as a stroke victim, don't worry, you haven't had one. You have fewer brain cells trying to do the same job. Everything from work to play is a lot more work. On top of that, the new you keeps insisting on your old performance and, as hard as you try, you just can't deliver.

But face it, pal, your brain injury has *been* delivered and the sooner you accept that as a fact of life, the better. Telling yourself that a lot of people have it worse is true, but it's not working is it? No, it's time to accept a brain injury like your height and quit wasting energy by moping about the damn thing.

Luckily, a brain injury is like your weight, and there's a lot you can do about that!

If you still think that the body and mind are separate mechanisms, think again. Any doctor will tell you they don't work separately and you can't improve one without the other. Having a brain injury means your body gets fewer and slower signals from your brain. They work together poorly, if at all. Every injury heals more slowly— from everyday cuts and scratches to sprained ankles; common headaches to appendicitis; routine bruises to life-threatening diseases.

Hopefully, you don't have any life-threatening diseases. But the skinned knees that used to get better without Band-Aids, the sore ankles that got better without Ace bandages and the colds that got better without drugs have become tedious ordeals, haven't they? This point can be made in a single sentence:

Healing any injured site requires millions of brain signals and injured brains send out fewer of them.

If fewer signals weren't enough aggravation, they make things worse by taking their time to arrive.

Think of yourself as the foreman of a smaller crew that's also lazy.

All this became clearer when I was released from the hospital. Sliding off my bed into a wheelchair, I was told that damn chair would be a reality until I could get around on crutches. As soon as I wheel-chaired though the lobby, I came face to face with feelings of inadequacy I will never forget.

When I got home, these feelings multiplied times 10. It seemed like I had to see a doctor every other day. It took six months before I could eat anything but baby food. It took a year before I could shower and shave by myself. It took two years before I could walk up my steep driveway. I was always getting lost. I developed night sweats. I had scary nightmares. My endurance was gone. I wanted to get everything over with as quickly as possible, especially eating.

The crash left me with a damaged throat. I'd always have to worry about food going down the wrong way and setting off an embarrassing coughing jag. This means that eating went from an opportunity to applaud Mary's cooking and talking with friends to a stress-test.

Eating was bad enough, but talking to friends over the dinner table was even worse, not to mention dealing with busy waiters in a busy restaurant. I even got embarrassed when I forgot that a server I'd known for years had been replaced.

I'm Dillon. Diesel doesn't work here anymore.

At home, I was constantly embarrassed by quick fits of useless anger. I kept forgetting why I came into certain rooms and what I was supposed to do when I got there. I'd forget my new friends' names and switch them with my old friends' names. I had delayed responses that made me feel like I was a new cartoon character called B-DUH-MAN.

It seemed like I was confronting some new failure every day. My short-term memory was gone and I was sure I was being ridiculed behind my back. I was constantly embarrassed by quick fits of useless anger.

Oh, did I just say that?

My mind felt totally mindless. I felt out of control. I never wanted to get out of bed. And if I made it out of bed, my butt would grow roots as soon as I sat in a chair. I felt like I had to have triple backups for everything because I didn't trust the universe anymore. When I couldn't find a sponge, I'd be furious. I kept talking to myself out loud. And every morning felt crankier than the last.

One appointment on my weekly schedule was all I could handle. I had to make everything conscious. There was never enough time to get things done. And I kept rehearsing simple conversations I planned to have with friends.

You've probably experienced all those feelings, not to mention these:

Everything makes you anxious. You have overreactions to tiny mistakes. You have an obsessive need to be perfect. You hate being alone. You lock doors for no good reason and you hate sudden noises.

You're not as practical as you used to be. You process new information too slowly. You're always lost in useless thought (this is also known as perseveration). You're always counting things for no reason. You're always doing things in the wrong order.

Beyond that, you have chronic short-term memory loss. Forgetting makes you angry. Holding things in your memory is hard work. You can't remember what you did in the morning after lunch. It's hard to remember what happened yesterday. Recent failures blot out recent successes.

You get tired after a good night's sleep. Early morning stress ruins your whole day. No amount of rest puts you in the positive column. Enough rest just keeps you out of the negative column. You often get a stunned feeling.

You probably also have rigid new rules. You get angry over nothing. You get into meaningless fights about computers, your relatives or her friends. Your angry moods last way too long.

You hate driving on curved roads. You're afraid of driving too fast. you're always scraping your car on the garage doorway.

Your arm keeps posturing like you've had a stroke. You're always knocking things over. New environments use so much energy your brain signals slow down and you get clumsy.

And if all that weren't enough, you worry about getting early Alzheimer's and often contemplate suicide.

So does this mean the new you'll have to give up coolness, self-control and warm relationships? We'll see about that.

Of course, your new mind isn't the only place that has trouble handing you difficulties. Your new body has challenges, too.

If you still see yourself breaking the tape at 10K's, charging through obstacle courses or kicking game-winning goals—good!

Those aren't my memories, but if they're yours, hang on to them, they'll come in handy. Just remember, your new brain signals are so lazy, you can't expect any movement to be what it used to be.

If you have tired eyes, if you feel dizzy whenever you make a fast move, if you get dizzy from straightening up or bending over—get used to it. If you get dizzy from running, biking or doing flip turns or if you get dizzy from making any fast twisting motion in the gym—get used to it, too. If you hate the way your own shadow moves—well, you know what I'm going to say. You're getting an early taste of old age and the slow brain signals that come with it.

Those slow brain signals may not bug you all the time, but they start worrisome chain reactions that are the facts of a brain-injured life.

Really slow brain signals cause vertigo, which causes injuries, which cause other injuries.

Slow brain signals cause the fluid in your inner ear to react too slowly, which causes bad balance. Bad balance causes sudden falls and sudden falls cause scrapes, bruises and dislocations. Whoopee! Your old injuries keep creating new ones!

So do slow brain signals mean the new you will have to say goodbye to smooth coordination, high-speed moves and lifting heavy weights? Do slow brain signals mean you have to get used to inertia? Do slow brain signals mean more boredom?

We'll see about that.

Chapter 6
New Guts, New Glory

I'd like to say I dumped my old idea of bravery as soon as I got out of the hospital. I'd like to say it came to me in my first shower. I'd like to say it only took a few years, but I'd be lying.

Like most of us, I grew up believing that Hollywood heroes were the real thing. Cowboys, soldiers, athletes, cops and private detectives. John Wayne, Humphrey Bogart and Superman; all the way to Clint Eastwood's Rowdy Yates in *Rawhide.*

After the crash, it took more than 10 years to dump my macho image of bravery. Ten years before I could admit I wasn't indestructible. Ten years before I could admit my new limitations were permanent. Ten years before I could even think about writing this book. Ten years to accept a new definition of bravery.

Hey, the first glimmerings of this new bravery even told me that the new me may not stink as bad as I thought it did.

This whole book is about redefining bravery, but first, some basic principles.

The most important of these was acceptance. Any kind of bravery was impossible until I accepted some basic new truths. My TBI condition was so hard to believe that overcoming these new obstacles seemed impossible at first. I kept thinking I was still the guy I always was.

As soon as I accepted my new conditions, another enemy was waiting to pounce.

Denial

If I'm really honest about it, acceptance is bravery and denial is cowardice. It was time to *deny denial and accept acceptance.*

Now bravery meant lasting through a long ordeal and putting up with a painfully slow recovery. It seemed like rewiring took forever.

Thoughts about suicide haunted me 24/7. As a result, bravery meant confronting and stamping them out every day of my life. Amazingly, this constant rejection of death actually helped me enjoy life.

I had to quit being embarrassed all the time.

Suddenly bravery meant not being ashamed about looking uncoordinated, seeming confused or being the constant center of attention. I just had to buck up and learn to live with my infirmities.

It was time to quit having ugly mood swings.

Back in the frontier days, the brave way to keep from screaming was biting down on a musket ball. Whenever I felt an ugly mood coming on, I would too.

Bad moods were not only bringing on depression, they were pissing off the very people who were trying to help me.

I thought I'd better stop worrying about my new eccentricities. It occurred to me that everybody's eccentric in one way or another. In fact, we're so used to it, nobody even notices any more. It was time to stop thinking of myself as weird. And, it was time to quit thinking of myself in a special class.

I had to stop being overly sensitive and jumpy from surprises.

Most people over-react and make them worse, but I wanted to quit being a scaredy-cat as soon as I could.

I stopped using crutches or aids of any kind. This has been a heavenly process, because the sooner I got rid of one, the sooner I never had to think about it again.

Bravery meant dumping my fear of risk. Taking risks took bravery for sure, but it turned out that just *trying* really was heroic enough. This really paid off because the more chances I took, the easier my routine became and, the sooner I got back in control.

Bravery came to mean having high standards.

High standards were harder to maintain, but they usually led to winning. Low standards, on the other hand, were easier, but they always led to failure.

Really low expectations became an enemy to run from and high expectations have been a friend to embrace.

My new definition of bravery has helped me travel more often. Good thing because I've come to realize that alien environments have actually helped me deal with familiar surroundings, and now I appreciate home even more.

Who knew that socializing would take the most bravery of all? I've never thought of partying as a heroic act, but the poise, cleverness and manners it took to be with groups scared me senseless.

Socializing was hard work at first, but the more I did it, the better I got at adlibbing. I'd like to say it also made me a more charming guy, but I'll leave that to others. By the way, there are some people I'll never be brave enough for and neither will you.

You don't need 10 years or anything like it. You can totally redefine your idea of bravery starting right now. It's time to kick those old heroic images right in the butt. It's time to get angry about creating your own obstacles. It's time to be less embarrassed about walking, talking, eating and playing. It's time to step off that lumbering old local and join me on the speedy express. It's time to zoom by other survivors without even slowing down. And it's high time to stop worrying about how you're coming off. Listen, you're probably making a much better impression than you think you are.

The dictionary defines bravery as courage, the quality of mind or spirit that enables a person to face difficulties like danger or pain without fear.

Fine. But that old definition doesn't work anymore does it?

No, your new definition shouldn't be about bravery in combat, rodeos or chasing the bad guys. It's time to give up going for ridiculous athletic records. It's time to face reality and be brave about reaching *achievable goals.*

Your new idea of bravery should be about removing obstacles. Obstacles like fatigue, forgetfulness and confusion. Obstacles like blowing your stack, awkwardness or clumsiness. Obstacles that are in your way. Obstacles that slow you down. Obstacles that cause detours and U-turns. Obstacles that give you sticky feet.

Ganesha is an ancient Hindu god who is worshipped and revered for his help in overcoming obstacles. And since TBIs create so many obstacles, it seems to me that you should at least be familiar with who he is.

O Lord Ganesha who has a large body, curved trunk and brightness of a million suns, please remove all obstacles in my work always.
HINDU PRAYER

Replacing my old heroes with "Ganesha-heroes" has really worked for me. Obstacles have been my main problem for 22 years, but Ganesha-heroes have inspired me to run further on jogging paths, lift more in the gym, be more graceful at the dinner table, smarter on the computer and listen more on the phone.

Obstacles, obstacles, obstacles. I had so many obstacles, my friend Chip got me a small Ganesha statue and I am looking at it right now.

Whenever I've been brave enough to be brave, it's worked for me. But that hasn't always been true.

I still have to run alone, I still go to the gym during off-peak hours and I still avoid any socializing that I can. Adaptation is still a constant struggle and worst of all, I'm still worried about losing my wife and friends.

My bravery isn't legendary by any means and I may not be the perfect role model, but I will say this: I have stopped wasting time on the above compromises and it's helped to have some Ganesha-heroes.

The way I see it, Ganesha-heroes don't give things up, they just keep working around their limitations.

Hey pal, our time on this planet is limited. It's time to accept your new condition, quit stalling and remember you'll need a new kind of guts to bask in a new kind of glory.

My new idea of bravery has helped me face some ugly new truths, get over my childlike embarrassment and become willing to talk about myself and tell my personal story.

Chapter 7
Rehab

Mary

There's not much information out there about rehab hospitals. Like most people, I didn't understand much about the therapy process. Not even enough to know what questions to ask.

The medical library had some information that was primarily technical, but there were a few useful tidbits. Regular news magazines also rank rehab hospitals nationwide now and then. I developed a list of questions to ask about their treatment programs. Apparently, football players and other famous people have numerous accidents and need help. The facilities they use receive publicity.

Friends had information, too. The nurses from ICU referred me to people who had been through our local rehab hospital and I talked with others who had been to mainland facilities.

One friend called with the name of an East Coast place. Phil's brother talked to a famous neurosurgeon in New York City. He had a suggestion or two. As I reviewed the catalog of rehab hospitals, I also looked at cities where I had friends and family to call on.

The therapists and physicians all knew where the best rehab facilities were. Some of the medical residents in ICU were heading to a world-famous rehab facility in southern California as a part of their training.

I finally got a solid list. It included the Rehabilitation Hospital of the Pacific located in Hawaii, five facilities in southern California and one in Colorado.

I wanted to get Phil out of the regular hospital fast.

Nothing takes the place of showing up, so I visited Rehab Hospital of the Pacific. It looked okay at the main entrance. The outpatient facility downstairs was all right. Overall, it was not the most modern of facilities, but it was adequately equipped for the basics.

But upstairs, the head injury ward was a horrible place. It resembled a crazy ward in an ancient, state-run institution. The walls needed painting. The equipment was antiquated. The patients frightened me to tears. This was worse than a crazy ward because half of the patients had parts of their skulls missing. Almost none could walk, even those who only had head injuries. There were people in restraining beds, and all along the corridor men and women were in wheelchairs, drooling, shouting and bobbing their heads. Their eyes seemed frozen in a wide-eyed "deer in the headlights" look.

Like Phil.

I took the whole tour and talked with administrators, physicians and therapists. There was lots of talk about restraint and the policies about the involvement of family members.

"You can't stay with him at night."

"We only use a camisole if absolutely required." (A camisole is the same thing as a straitjacket—shades of *One Flew Over the Cuckoo's Nest*.)

"One member of the family is required to assist at all therapy sessions."

I went home, sat in the corner of the room on the floor, hugged my knees and cried. Reality check. I didn't understand anything about head injuries. I wanted to take Phil to a place that looked nice, had state-of-the-art equipment and strong staffing. A place that wouldn't send you into deep depression.

Scouting them myself seemed to be the only way I could understand the options, so I planned a trip to Southern California and Colorado to see how other rehab hospitals looked.

My first concern was who was going to take care of Phil while I was gone. I called around. Our families were already dealing with operations and hospitalizations on the East Coast. Things weren't good on the home front.

Friends came to the rescue. Tim took vacation time to come to Queen's hospital. George and Richard came with him. It was like leaving Phil with the Marx Brothers—they were all smart, funny and kind of goofy.

Leaving Phil was unbelievably difficult. Even though I had three close friends to take care of him in the daytime and a professional nurse for the evenings, I was still worried.

Anyway, there didn't seem to be any other option. I had five days to check out five facilities spread out over Southern California and in Colorado plus get to and from Hawaii. Five days for a crash course in rehab hospitals!

Los Angeles proved to be a wonderful break. I slept all night. Between appointments, I spoke with friends, ran on the beach, drank designer coffee and looked for a wedding dress for my friend, Brier.

Driving around Southern California searching for the perfect rehab center was a huge relief and yet I felt guilty. I felt so guilty that I could escape my situation and that Phil couldn't.

The phone calls were all that we had. They were heartbreaking. Phil would struggle to speak, yet Tim told me how excited and agitated he became when we talked.

Touring the rehab hospitals wasn't easy. People recovering from head injuries are pitiful. Their families are in shock. Everyone involved was as stunned as I was.

Rehab hospitals are not attractive. Many are located in old buildings with lots of large ward settings with 10 or more beds to a room. After visiting the facilities in Southern California, I realized that there was no way to make rehab from a head injury "pretty." It's an ugly business and the best you can hope for is an energetic, positive staff.

The measure of a good facility became how the staff and facility managed. Were they energetic and enthusiastic or did the place feel like a morgue? Was the administration able to provide a positive environment in the face of extreme challenges or was the staff angry and irate about policy? I didn't have to ask. It was obvious from walking through the therapy rooms.

The hospital administrators and admissions personnel were not used to dealing with people like me. They were not prepared for a lot of involvement by the patient's family. There was a lot of "We don't deal with patients and their families directly, we only talk to physicians." What I told them was, they could talk to the physician all they wanted, but if I didn't approve of their facility, Phil would not be going there.

My list of questions was long and pretty complete, but there were still questions that I wish I'd spent more time asking.

Touring helped me understand the impact TBIs have on balance, coordination and the ability of the muscles to function. TBIs take a long time to heal. A head injury was a much bigger deal than I had thought.

As I looked at people one and two years down the path of recovery and saw how far they still had to go to reach "normal," I began to understand the magnitude of the challenge that Phil and I were facing. Not only were Phil's physical injuries severe, the injury to the brain compounded the problem times 10. We had a huge job ahead.

The decision regarding where to go for rehabilitation came down to:

- a facility in South Central Los Angeles where we would be prisoners to the neighborhood due to the high crime rate.
- a facility 80 miles outside Los Angeles—a long way from friends.
- the Rehabilitation Hospital of the Pacific on Oahu. I didn't have the best feeling about it, but it was close to home. The weather was easy, warm, the people friendly. No travel required.

I began to believe that rehab was not where Phil was going to recover. However, it was the place where he would gain weight and a little strength. It seemed like a place for me to learn to take care of Phil and manage his recovery.

My strategy shaped up to be less about Phil and more about me. Phil was so exhausted and weak that all he could handle was the minimum. I, on the other hand, could deal with it 24 hours a day.

An ambulance took Phil from Queen's to the Rehab Hospital of the Pacific.

Dressing Phil was our first activity. It took over an hour to get three pieces of clothing on him. He was skinny—size 29 shorts were baggy. His face was pale, gaunt and caught in a perpetual look of surprise. Plus, he had a hospital scissors haircut.

At last, Phil had his first rehab evaluation. Head injuries are measured on the Rancho Los Amigos Scale of Cognitive Functioning. He was on Level V out of VI.

Phil had an attention span of a minute or two. He gave the year as 1992, the month as March, the place as New York and his age as three. He thought he was in prison. More than two or three people in the room made him anxious.

He remembered details from New York and New Jersey but these were mixed up with Hawaii, London, Los Angeles and East Hampton, where he had weekended and vacationed for 10 years. He couldn't remember who I was.

The brain injury had serious affects on his body. The left side of his face, mouth and throat were paralyzed. His left side was spastic. His balance was affected. Sleep was erratic.

Phil's left leg was still in a long leg cast. His right leg was in a brace to stabilize the right knee. His left arm was unresponsive. His right arm was weak and shook. His left shoulder was swollen. He had a feeding tube in his stomach. He was dependent on others for everything.

In the first days Phil was in a zippered bed. He was too weak to move and frightened by the confining bed.

The theory is to provide head injury patients with measurable steps of improvement. All head injury patients start in the zippered bed. When they prove themselves to be trustworthy, they are promoted to a regular bed, a sign of graduation and a way to avoid straitjackets at night.

This wasn't what I would have done, but we were paying for their expertise.

Therapy took place in bed during the first week. Initially, physical therapy consisted of sitting practice, instruction in the use of the transfer board (used to move Phil from the bed to the wheelchair) and the therapist tossing a beach ball at Phil to see if he could bat it away and not fall over. Ten minutes was a long session.

Occupational therapy consisted of relearning the use of utensils and pens by gripping a spoon with an enlarged handle and a fat pen. Phil's writing was large and unintelligible. Not that his handwriting was that legible before, but it had been smaller.

Speech therapy worked on swallowing and orientation. A session consisted of his eating pureed baby food to retrain his throat muscles to swallow again. Then there was answering questions about where he was, what day it was, how old he was, what was his address, etc. In a good session he remembered the date within a year or two.

Other major tasks involved getting Phil in and out of the wheelchair, in and out of bed, as well as grooming and bathing. Everything was an effort. The transformation from an athletic adult male to a "baby" was scary.

After the first week, life began to look up. He was moved into a hospital bed and therapy moved into the therapy room. There were two sessions of each type of therapy each day. A difficult morning session was followed by easier activities in the afternoon. The big activity in physical therapy was to get Phil walking again. Walking was an activity that the athlete in him could relate to.

When you learn to walk, you start on a tilt table. The tilt table is exactly what it sounds like. It's a table that the patient is strapped onto in a flat horizontal position and then the table and the patient are tilted slowly to a standing position. The tilt table worked on blood pressure—after lying down for three months, standing up would have caused him to pass out. The tilt table also stretched out his right Achilles tendon. That tendon had been stretched many times a day, but was still atrophied. The tilt table fixed that.

The therapist started Phil with one minute at an angle between standing and lying. It was a long, painful minute. "Go! Go! Go! Just a few more seconds, Phil. Don't give up." There were grimaces, pain, sweat and focus. His willpower helped a lot. Phil's success on the tilt table inspired the other patients.

When he was finally upright, his hands weren't capable of rolling a walker forward. Extenders allowed him to use his armpits and body weight to walk. First a few feet, then twenty feet, then 20 feet, then 40 feet. The cheering that accompanied his progress sounded like an English soccer match. The intensity of the effort was Olympic.

Speech therapy was a mixed bag. It was great when he got the right answer, but awful when he didn't know that an apple was a fruit, or a tree was a plant. I tried to help with the answers by rolling my eyes at the wrong answer, encouraging the right one and arguing over the ambiguous questions. One ambiguous example was a picture of a man in a white coat with a tongue depressor. Phil identified him as a doctor. The therapist said, "No, he's an Otorhinolaryngologyst."

I was not convinced that this effort was worth it. Time appeared to help Phil's speech more than therapy, and the condescending attitude of the therapists riled both of us.

Occupational therapy focused on arm motion and grooming, primarily teaching me to groom Phil. I learned the tricks of the shower stall, particularly the getting in and out of it. I learned about shower seats and learned to keep the leg cast dry. There was range-of-motion work. Large rubber grips were used around pencils and forks. Eventually, he practiced putting pegs in holes and pulling on rubber bands.

Occupational therapy baffled me. Phil's major muscles didn't have the strength to support fine-motor movement. His arms were too weak to hold a comb. Why weren't we working on overall strength?

The days were long. After therapy, there were over 20 hours left in the day. Getting outside became our relief. Phil's legs were stretched in front of him. Maneuvering around was a bit like driving a Lincoln Continental. We were always executing Y-turns. We'd tip the chair back to relieve the pressure and hang out by a picnic table with Phil's feet high in the air and his head on my shoulder.

We hung out at the obstacle course between naps and therapy sessions. A steep ramp led to the 100-foot oval course. Obstacles had been placed there to train wheelchair operators to handle life in the real world. There were ramps, curbs, soft ground, gravel, sand, grass and asphalt. Heavily-scented puakenikeni trees were planted along the walk and a large net had been set up for golf practice. Two tennis courts provided a small, protected place where we waited out the afternoon rain.

Some of our difficulties in the rehab hospital had to do with false economies, like the debacle over the catheter. The nurses were required to use a large, cheap catheter. It caused pain and an infection. When I insisted, a smaller catheter that cost 50 cents more was used. Any savings from the large catheter had to be spent on antibiotics to treat the urinary tract infection.

Another example of the hospital saving costs was the reduced staffing situation at night. Phil didn't want us to leave him at night. Something was happening at night that troubled him. He had my phone number and I told the staff he could call anytime he wanted. When he could get a nurse, the night nurse would dial and Phil would speak. He wasn't easy to understand. The words were unintelligible, incomprehensible.

The night staff at the rehab hospital had problems being understood as well. Most were new immigrants with limited English. It was a communications disaster because Phil and the nurses couldn't understand each other. The high point of their understanding was coming hourly to ask if he had to go to the bathroom.

At night the staff to patient ratio puts the staff in overdrive when their minds and bodies are in underdrive, all at a time when the patients need more attention.

One night I woke up dreaming Phil was calling for me. Something bad was happening. No one answered my telephone call, so I rushed to the hospital. When I arrived, there were screams, yells and buzzers coming from rooms up and down the hall. The nurses were standing in the nursing station preparing charts, shuffling papers.

Phil was one of those people yelling. He was sitting on the floor in his room, his legs out in front. The nurses didn't hear a thing.

The second night Phil fell out of bed, they wanted to put him in a straitjacket. The staff felt he was trying to escape. Escape to where? There were threats of putting him back in the zippered bed or worse. What was happening? He had tried to pull himself into a sitting position. The weight of the cast on his left leg slid him right out of bed. Escape? He just needed to relieve the pressure on his bony back.

After the second fall, I spent nights in his room.

On the first night I stayed, drugs were administered at 10:00 P.M. I had settled down in my chair with a blanket and pillow and drifted off. Phil woke me. He was yelling, "Get the fire off of me." He screamed about guerrillas coming down the hall and killing everyone. Didn't I see the flames?

For him, *Apocalypse Now* was happening right there in the rehab hospital. The effects of his bad drug took eight hours to wear off. No wonder Phil was exhausted during the day. He had been up all night fighting a war. Why hadn't we known the drugs were doing this before? The nursing staff was supposed to check on him every hour.

The staff didn't question whether or not the drugs should be administered in light of his reaction. I spoke to his doctor. After that, we refused all drugs except analgesics.

My spending the night meant we sat in the dark together, talking, resting with my head on the bed next to Phil. I didn't worry about him being alone anymore. Phil didn't have to be frightened. I was grateful to be with him. He was grateful to be with me.

Holidays in a hospital are a must miss. That Christmas there seemed to be dozens of choral groups and Santas. After the first few, we began to resent the emotional trauma of being reminded over and over again that we weren't at home.

By contrast, secret champagne and illicit food were a must. Over Christmas our friends and family had more time to spend with us. My parents came for a month. We had company from the Big Island. It was great to laugh, catch up on the world. Had we heard about the fire at Kohala Ranch? How about the big drug bust? We found out Leo and Megan were moving in early summer. Chelsea danced a Christmas hula.

During the holidays the hospital goes into survival mode. There are fewer therapists, fewer nurses and no administrators. On holidays, an all-day outing is recommended.

We had been invited to join friends for their family celebration—imagine how kind it was to share their Christmas Day. It took a vanload of equipment, everything from a Port-O-Let to a blender.

But finally, Phil was sitting in a lawn chair with a giant foam pad right by the ocean looking out toward Black Point and Diamond Head. He got to spend a warm, sunny day near the ocean, with his Santa hat, his Christmas shirt and their Saint Bernard sitting right next to him.

Being there on Christmas Day was like going from hell to heaven. The hospitality was relaxed and caring and the setting was exquisite. Difficulties with mobility, bathrooms, food and energy seemed to be handled with grace and dignity. It was the best Christmas of my life. I had Phil. He was alive. We were out of the hospital, if even just for a few hours.

Outings weren't easy. There were endless logistics to deal with of which the biggest was the bathroom. There were also stairs, curbs, the length of Phil's extended leg, the width of the wheelchair and in general, the pace of the world.

For one of our practice outings, we went to the Honolulu Zoo where, for most people, looking at Phil was more interesting than looking at the animals.

The world was moving faster than we were, but it looked great to us. Our impatience to get out of the rehab hospital grew. The hospital seemed more and more inane and bureaucratic.

I felt their strategy for working with Phil was inappropriate and the staff inadequate. Egg Beaters arrived looking like soup every morning. There was no one to help get Phil out of bed in the morning. Other patients screamed all night.

The attitude of the staff was driving me crazy. They said things like, "Oh, Phil, you'll never be any better so why try too hard?"

"You're in denial, dear. Better to learn to live with it than fight it."

"His memory will never get any better, you know, between age and the accident."

"Better start planning for the future. He'll always be this way."

I saw their job as energizers, idea people, encouragers, teachers but they didn't see it that way. Phil was not a baby or an idiot. He was a recovering athlete. We needed action, not psychiatric help.

We began to take responsibility for the situation. If the professionals weren't up to it, we'd have to make our own way.

Am I being fair? Maybe not. Maybe expecting rehabilitation to help you do more than just get by is expecting too much. Maybe other patients and families just want to get by. Not us.

The administrative problems surrounding the accident were causing me anxiety. Bills were arriving, but our health insurance company wasn't going to pay them unless we agreed to reimburse them first if we received any other insurance money. The cost of the accident appeared to be over $500,000. That meant our policy left over $100,000 in medical bills for us to pay. If the drunk driver's insurance company paid any money for the accident, it would all go to our health insurance company and we would be left with $100,000 in medical bills. It was time for the lawyers.

Getting home felt like the answer—home where our life was. In order to get home, I needed Phil to help me transfer him to and from the wheelchair. It took two people to move him from the bed and he was getting heavier. For us to be independent, he had to help me.

No matter how much I wanted to leave, the insurance company had us tethered to the hospital until Phil was strong enough to leave. They would pay hundreds of dollars a day for ineffective treatment in the hospital and would not pay to have help at home.

By mid-January we planned a move to a local hotel. From there we would bus back and forth to rehab for outpatient therapy until Phil was stronger. I counted the days and hours until we were out of "jail" and on our own. Until we were making our own mistakes and doing it our own way.

Day 105.

No more screaming in the halls. No more bars on the beds. No more strange plastic pads. No more security cameras. No more disinfectant smells. No more dark dank room. No more green walls. No more chipped linoleum floors. No more nurses. No more hospitals. No more ugliness.

Free at last.

A king-size bed. Holding each other. Just clean, crisp sheets and soft pillows. Windows open. The smell of the ocean. The sound of the boats, the cars, the airplanes, the noise of the city. Beautiful light all around.

The coastline. The ocean in the distance. Waves rolling in. The city and all its lights below. Honolulu! Waikiki!

Food. Real, tasty food. A room-service feast. Pureed for Phil since he still couldn't swallow well enough for regular food. Black bean soup with bananas. Fresh fruit. Flan. Kiawe-grilled salmon.

Carpeted floors. Regular furniture that didn't buzz or roll. A couch! Tables!

A hotel! Not quite home. A half-way house between an institution and home. Not the hospital and not home. The Twilight Zone.

We needed to stay in Oahu for follow-up medical care and additional therapy sessions. Phil still had a long leg cast. He was several weeks away from a shorter one that would make us more mobile. The doctors were still following the blood clot in Phil's neck. And Phil still wasn't strong enough to help me move him. But moving out of the hospital meant taking a big step towards normality.

Even though Phil was a long way from better, both of us wanted to get rid of the signs of illness, like the giant blue foam pad. No sleeping on polyester foam pads ever again. Second to go was the attitude that Phil was strictly a patient. He wanted to help out, be involved, be athletic and participate in life again.

Wanting did not make it so. Phil needed 100 percent assistance for all grooming, self-care, eating and moving. There was nothing he could do on his own. All the jobs that I had shared with nurses were now mine with the help of family and friends.

Bathing was the most difficult of these tasks. We bathed Phil every day. Each morning about 5:00 A.M., when Phil couldn't lie in bed a second longer, we would head for the bathtub. Bathing, shaving and dressing. We could have eased up on the schedule—a bath every other day, perhaps—but Phil wanted to look good and looking good is a key part of feeling good.

Adapting to Phil's physical disabilities was strictly trial and error. Food preparation. Energy management. Sleep. Walks in the park. Getting in and out of a car. When we made mistakes or something didn't work, we tried something else. As long as we were in the hospital, we had to play by their rules. As soon as we got out, we could do what we wanted. And we did.

Electric stimulation, massage, extra protein and supplement drinks. We did them all. It was our show now. We were taking the responsibility for Phil's recovery.

He worked hard at four therapy sessions a week when we went back to the hospital. The sessions got tougher for him as he became more aware. The tone and tenor of the therapists was still condescending. The content of the sessions was not challenging. And they didn't appreciate Phil's sense of humor.

The highlight of therapy continued to be physical therapy. Both the therapist and Phil were willing to try anything. When Phil started at the outpatient clinic, he could walk 40 feet with a walker that had high extensions. By the time he left, he could walk for short distances with a four-pronged cane. Phil worked so hard that he inspired other patients. He worked himself to exhaustion. It took four massage sessions a week to rub out the stiffness and get him back to another therapy session.

He never complained about pain. Even when he was sweating and pale, he never said, "Yes, I hurt." In his view, if he admitted to any discomfort at all, it would have meant he was dying. He *did* have pain. Shingles appeared on his torso. Every night he had abdominal cramps from the imbalance of his long-leg cast. He woke almost every hour with a stiff and sore body, but he never complained!

Phil never said he was dizzy either. You could see he was dizzy by the way he rocked around when he sat up or stood up. But if you asked him, it was no problem.

Phil didn't want anyone to see him in a wheelchair (hard to do when that's your main mode of transportation). When friends came to visit, he made sure he was standing holding onto the windowsill when they arrived. Only then was it okay to return to the wheelchair.

Television was too confusing and violent for him to watch. The evening news was too harsh for him. The Los Angeles earthquake was frightening. He couldn't look at the images. He was too vulnerable, the accident was too fresh. The loss of certainty in life was too new.

Ala Moana Breach Park in Honolulu proved to be our savior. All the long, yawning gaps of time that we had were filled in this park. Wheeling Phil around. Sitting and watching skaters and joggers and strollers go by. Showing up to see the outrigger clubs start their afternoon practice sessions. Hanging out on the breakwater watching the waves roll in. Being out in the sunshine made us feel free of the hospital, even though we were a long way from being free of the accident.

Nights were hellish. Wake-ups happened hourly. Waking up to use the bathroom. Waking up with stomach spasms. Waking up in total confusion. Sleep deprivation like this put an ugly edge on the daylight hours.

Bills and nasty letters arrived from the insurance company. Collection agencies started to call. The legal process took forever. For a while nothing was happening—except trouble.

Meanwhile, the rehab hospital was showing a tape to patients to prepare them for their future. It was from the National Head Injury Foundation and the tape was designed as a fundraiser. This piece presented a series of poor, struggling victims of head injuries, people who were gallantly coping with horrible disabilities—hardly the uplifting, motivating piece to send us out into the real work of the recovery. Apparently, the attitude of the staff was to prepare the patients to get used to living with their head injury for the rest of their lives.

Their attitude was inconsistent with what I was seeing in the real world. People approached me, strangers who saw Phil and wanted to share positive stories. They talked about their own accidents 10 to 15 years earlier when they had had serious head injuries, severe structural damage and rehab facilities weren't available. And today, you would never know they had had an accident. That was us!

Why didn't the rehab hospital show a video of people who successfully recovered, something to encourage others to do the hard work to get better? Why work so hard to induce a frightened, defeated mental state?

I didn't feel like there was much help anywhere. Organized, authorized therapy looked less and less useful. Friends couldn't live with us forever. Lawyers couldn't take care of the daily bill-collector calls. And I was the only one taking care of Phil at night.

The stress was catching up. When Phil was too exhausted to go to therapy, I got angry. I was angry at rehab. I was angry at the drunk. I was angry about the loss of our lives. I was angry that no one was there to love and touch me. I was angry at God.

Crying jags happened. Running was the only time when the tension was released. I ran every day to keep from going crazy. Talking helped too. I spread my complaints around to all our friends to ease the pressure.

Home was where I wanted to be and home was where Phil wanted to be, but home scared me. It was not only 15 miles from the nearest town, it was miles from the nearest neighbor. Going home would mean Phil and I would be alone.

Chapter 8
Get Mad

It's often said you don't get better until you get mad about staying in bed. That must be true, because back in my hospital days, getting mad worked big time.

I got so annoyed at the stream of sympathetic visitors, sorrowful looks and corny get well cards, I wanted to scream. I got so mad at the bad food, moaning patients, constant blood pressure checks and endless status reports, I did scream.

I got so annoyed at the tours of eager medical students, the constant X-rays and mysterious medications in little paper cups, I wanted to stand up and shout. I got so pissed off about rolling over for new sheets, hearing fake apologies and smelling disinfectant, I did stand up and shout.

That was the first time I realized how much getting mad helps with a recovery. It helped me shake off the hospital routine. It helped me find my voice and it got me back on my feet! It helped me return to the guy I used to be.

I'd like to say I threw off my blankets and walked out of there forever, but the regulations said I had to wheelchair out.

My anger about being dependent made me so hungry to be independent that I rolled down the hall, through the reception room and out of those double doors forever.

If you're slamming more doors, starting more arguments, kicking the furniture, yelling at the dog and flashing the bird in daily bouts of road-rage—relax, pal, that kind of raw anger will come in handy one day.

If you're tailgating slow drivers, honking at crosswalks, having fits in restaurants, throwing hammers, kicking your garbage can and punching the wall—it's okay, all you need is better anger management.

If you're blowing your cool in front of friends, relatives, roommates, co-workers and complete strangers—stay tuned, all you need is a little more damage control.

Start by putting your apologies on hold and changing your attitude. Anger is nothing to be ashamed of. In fact, starting today, anger should become your best friend. And pal, a friend you need is a friend indeed.

It's as simple as this: *anger is a great motivator.* There's just nothing like red-hot fury to speed your recovery. You just need to think of it as another tool in your recovery kit and learn how to use it.

You're really not mad at other drivers, doors, furniture and appliances. You're really just mad at yourself. You're hopping mad about memory loss, confusion, outbursts and limitations. And who says you should never get mad at those things?

Not me. Getting mad got me going. It gave me the guts to dump my old self and overcome the challenges that led to a whole new outlook. Not to mention the balls to finish this book.

But anger is far from a new victory technique. Athletes of all kinds work up a kind of shadow-anger before they take the field. Football players do padding-slams in the locker room. Coaches enrage their teams at halftime. Tennis pros give each other the evil eye across the court and golfers swear at each other under their breath.

The best example of all comes from the fight game. Boxers not only get mad before fights, they use their anger to make strong attacks, shake off good punches and get up after knockdowns. But getting mad helps boxers do a lot more than stand up and keep punching. It reconfirms their former glories. It highlights their aggressive instincts. It restores their self-confidence and, most importantly, it helps them win the fight.

Think about it. Anger is a positive force you should greet with open arms because it signals the return of your own self-worth. Self-worth that can't be seen in a mirror, but you know it's there.

So it pays to get mad—you just have to change what you're getting mad at. I was ready to murder that drunk driver for years. I fantasized about it constantly. Then I realized that it was really a police problem and I'd let him become more important to me than my own goals. Even though I'll never forgive that drunken bastard, I'm sick and tired of being distracted and wasting hard-won energy on him. When I heard he drank himself to death in Germany, my immediate reaction was to shout, *Great! I'm glad that bastard's dead!*

This rampant anger used to come on as fast as hitting my thumb with a hammer. But thanks to smarter anger and the new goals that came with it, my aim got better when it came to throwing it away (see more on this in *Chapter 16: New Goals*).

Anyway, as natural as it is to get angry in life, sooner or later it pays to get a grip by accepting the truth. Accepting your new

TBI helps by helping you fight depression. There are a bunch of reasons for this, but the best one is: depression sucks!

Literally.

Depression will vacuum your hard-won initiatives, drives and desires right into a disposable dust bag. When you're depressed, you're sitting around feeling sorry for yourself. You're stuck in the boo-hoo zone. You're in flight mode, for sure.

But when you're angry, your adrenaline puts you back in *fight* mode ASAP. Think about it—angry responses are much more action oriented. You're throwing, kicking, yelling, fighting and playing offense, instead of apologizing, looking sheepish, feeling wimpy and playing defense.

When you're angry, you feel more intense, more dynamic and a lot more like doing something about it. You feel like you've had a booster shot of energy—because you have. You feel re-wired because you are.

Nothing rewires the brain's signals like the intense energy that comes from anger. It forces your newly rewired signals to create new neural pathways, pathways that grow around the dead cells and get the same jobs done. Your dead brain cells will never live again, but the concentrated power and electricity that floods your brain from getting mad will activate them again. Anger actually helps to create new routes around dead cells that work almost as well as they did when they were alive and well.

Taking the anger prescription means you won't win any popularity contests, but there's always time for that.

TBI symptoms never go away completely and getting a grip on your new TBI behavior is a life-long problem, so never get mad at being mad. It's a problem that should make you as mad as hell forever. The human brain is miraculous and later we'll discuss how smarter anger can help you rediscover your best self and bring it back to life.

It's taken me years to make my anger productive and it's only a matter of time until you'll be skipping the flight mode and embracing the fight mode, too. Pretty soon you and I may even have the same mantra:

Goddammit, this is not *okay.*

Chapter 9
Stalling

Now that you know the new you stinks and you've gotten mad enough to do something about it, it's time to what we all do.

STALL.

In spite of high-tech brain scans, the latest verbal tests and expert advice from qualified doctors, I simply couldn't admit I was less of a guy than I was six weeks ago. As soon as I got home from the hospital it got even realer.

Even though I had lots of concrete proof, I couldn't help telling myself the same thing over and over:

Goddammit, there's no way in hell this is me.

There's more. Whenever my stopwatch would tell me I was a slower runner, I would have to say:

Well, at least I'm running.

Whenever I thought my writing sessions were too short, I would have to say:

Hey, fifty words are better than nothing.

And since my literary, athletic and memory levels kept improving a little, I was sure my brain injury would disappear any day now.

Great, I thought, *maybe there's no need to work at getting better.*

STALLING.

Every morning I stayed busy writing essays and business books. I took a shot at the great American novel. I told myself that reading B-grade mysteries and movies weren't a waste of time because they were good fodder for writers.

MORE STALLING.

Even plateaus didn't help me confront the truth. I kept believing that running, swimming and weight lifting were too goal-oriented to be called procrastination.

When I got to the end of my obsessive six-day schedule, I took Sunday off because I was sure I deserved it.

Even though the old me was becoming a distant memory and the new me was a current reality, I did anything I could to keep from admitting that fact.

If this sounds familiar, you should know it took me years to quit stalling and write this sentence:

Hi. My name is Phil and I have a serious brain injury.

Call me the prince of procrastination.

Nothing new here. In college I majored in procrastination. Whenever I was supposed to get serious about hitting the books, I would hit on a cool girl instead.

Then whenever I'd get serious about a girl, I thought I'd better hit the books.

Stalling 101.

Whenever I'd get out of shape, I'd wait for lacrosse practice to start.

Intermediate stalling.

The same was true of smoking. Back in the 1960s, the cancer findings weren't a home truth yet, but everyone knew smoking brought on more colds and sinus infections. We all knew it was easier to quit sooner than later. Lucky for us college smokers, good old reliable procrastination kept us from admitting we were hooked on nicotine.

First, I told myself I'd keep smoking until the lacrosse season started. Then, I'd tell myself I'd quit after finals. Sometimes I'd tell some friend it was just a matter of days.

One day in a bar I actually pulled the plunger on the cigarette machine, tapped the pack, lit up and took a drag. I did this without remembering how any of it happened—it was completely unconscious! That unconscious act made me accept I was hooked and made me so mad I crumpled up the pack and decided to quit.

Advanced stalling.

Years later, I became a professional staller in the advertising business. I still remember that whenever I got a creative assignment, I'd find some administrative work that just couldn't wait. And whenever I had administrative work that just couldn't wait, I'd say, "This is bullshit, I'm really a creative guy."

Yuppie stalling.

These days I'm still at it. I begin every project by telling myself that I may not be able to see it through.

Literary stalling.

Procrastination may be natural, but if you keep stalling by denying you have a brain injury, you'll never recover.

If you keep ignoring brain scans, test results and medical advice, you'll never move on. If you keep living on earlier memories, you won't have to grow old because you'll already be old. If you keep relying on your old successes, if you keep avoiding new attempts, if you keep sticking to half-truths, if you keep hoping the old you will come back, if you keep seeing what you want to see, hearing what you want to hear and believing what you want to believe, your life will become a joke with a bad punch line.

In spite of these warnings, everybody stalls when they have to deal with bad news like being diagnosed with a TBI.

Especially me.

I'd like to quit stalling, but I just can't help it. Every time I need another medical test, I stall for days. Every time I'm due for another brain scan, I stall for weeks. And back when the experts said I needed psychological tests, I'd stall for months. Hey, the truth is I'm still stalling when it comes to any kind of doctor appointment.

But, in the end, my best role model turned out to be me. The wrong route eventually led me to the right route and I finally decided to quit procrastinating and jot down a new program that works for the new me. As soon as you quit stalling, you should do that, too.

The new you stinks and the old you is never coming back, so quit stalling. The new you is the *real* you and the time to accept that is right now!

Chapter 10
Home

Mary

Returning to the Big Island with a wheelchair, a walker, a Port-O-Let, a shower seat, a four-pronged cane and three boxes of aids was a gruesome change from months earlier. Before the accident, Phil would have needed a surfboard, a snowboard, a mountain bike, or a pair of running shoes to travel.

Phil's body was as different as his equipment. His legs didn't bend enough to get into a coach seat. His left arm was bent at the elbow and tightly clutched to his body. He was so skinny, he looked like mere skin and bones. He didn't know where he was or where we were going. He needed the hydraulic lift to exit the plane in Kona. And, the rain was streaming from the sky as we rolled across the tarmac.

Neither pictures or descriptions had jogged Phil's memory of our friends, our home or our lives. He kept asking questions like, "Where are we going?" and "Where's my mom?"

I was worried. Was the house okay? How much work would it take to shape it up? Could I take care of Phil on a rural island?

As we got near Kona's airport gate, we could see a crowd of friends waiting in the pouring rain. They had gathered to welcome us home. They not only had friendly signs and leis and smiles, they were soaking wet.

Tears flowed. Someone picked up the luggage and equipment. Someone else grabbed us and drove us home. Phil was packed with blankets and pillows in the back of our Trooper. He couldn't remember a thing. He kept asking the same questions over and over. He had lost all the memories of the four years we'd had together in Hawaii. Phil still wasn't even sure who I was. I couldn't even imagine his confusion.

A banner over the door welcomed us home. With his arms around me, Phil and I somehow got inside. When the door swung open, I could see the living room was filled with flowers. A comfortable chair we'd bought the week before was set up in the living room. The refrigerator was full of food we could both eat. The kitchen was full of flowers. Ramps had been installed over the step to the garage. The bedroom was full of flowers. Handles were on the bathroom walls. Firewood was stacked by the front door. Our friends had made our house a home again. And Phil finally began to remember.

What a relief to be back! Our own belongings, our own bed and lots of room to move around.

For the first two weeks we had help getting settled and figuring out the logistics of life. Then we were alone for the first time in months! That first month was grueling. The house was larger than the hotel room and Phil's arms were screaming with pain from the extra distances he had to get around with his walker. His legs were exhausted. And, when he called, sometimes I couldn't even hear him.

He was also freezing because the head injury had upset his internal thermometer. He would dress in sweats and pile, I would cover him with blankets and there was a fire burning continuously. Even in the tropics he was always shivering.

The routines I established on Oahu had to change. I had to help get Phil over the step into the shower. There were calls every time he needed to stand up, move around or go to the bathroom. Calls to help recline the recliner. Calls from just being fearful or fatigued.

He needed a hose instead of a showerhead. He needed chairs, rails and special seats for the john. I was looking though lots of special-equipment catalogs that would help him be independent as soon as possible.

What followed were months of painful endurance. Phil awoke every hour. At 4:00 A.M. he would get out of bed. He needed help in the bathroom and help with the heater. I had to prep and light the fireplace, help him shower and shave, brush his teeth. Get him to the living room, poke the fire, purée food. Feed him.

Then, more bathroom. Morning naps. Out for activities. Purée lunch and feed him again. Afternoon nap. Clean up. Help him back to the living room. Fan the fire. Make dinner. Purée dinner. Shower again. Brush teeth. Go to sleep. Get up every hour. And, on it went.

There were screaming fits of anger and frustration as Phil tried and tried and tried, but couldn't get out of the chair when he wanted. Or when he would choke on food or fall down or descend into the daily battle with the hiccups. At first the anger and wild cursing sessions were extremely stressful for both of us. One day after a particularly colorful rant, he looked to me like Yosemite Sam. Our inside joke became "sacafrasa-perka-shorka-bat-flattin'-portin-filabunkabertin', perkalooma burtin' dirtin' boostinattin' bartin' anatom."

Phil was working hard to adapt to the new environment. But he wanted to be himself again and dealing with his environment wasn't going to get him there.

Using my journals to keep track of Phil's progress helped us focus.

Day 140.	Standing without using hands.
Day 143.	Knees bend enough for a ride in the truck.
Day 148.	Unaided steps across the room.
Day 149.	Visit to the ocean.
Day 161.	Regular food.
Day 162.	Solo shave with an electric razor.
Day 168.	Took a dish to the kitchen without dropping it.
Day 171.	Able to get out of his chair alone.
Day 176.	Walked a quarter mile in 22 minutes.
Day 187.	Solo trip to the bathroom.
Day 188.	Got into car without help.
Day 188.	Walked without a cast.
Day 189.	Remembered a drunk driver did this.
Day 193.	100 pounds blaster squats. 30 pounds bench press.
Day 198.	Lay down on a surfboard.
Day 200.	Poured himself a cup of coffee.
Day 201.	Fell down. Got up alone.
Day 202.	Stretch session.
Day 215.	Undressed himself.
Day 219.	Mainland airline flight.
Day 223.	Movie in a movie theater.
Day 226.	Left arm straightened.
Day 233.	Opened the front gate alone.
Day 243.	Solo supervised shower.
Day 248.	Solo dressing.
Day 259.	Sword class.
Day 263.	Remembered a dream!
Day 273.	No walking stick!
Day 276.	Solo shave with his Gillette razor.
Day 282.	Climbed down a ladder into the pool.

Day 287.   Turned over on a lounge chair by himself.
Day 298.   Flossed teeth.
Day 302.   Half a lap in the pool.
Day 307.   Carried surfboard to the beach.
Day 309.   Full lap in the pool.
Day 316.   Catch with a baseball and a mitt, too. Drove around the driveway.
Day 351.   Left thumb touched other fingers on the left hand.
Day 354.   Unsupervised shower. Two hours alone.

Rehabilitation and recovery were the real challenge. Phil had to keep building strength and regaining use of his limbs. The local rehab clinic was our establishment option. The facility looked nicer than the rehab hospital but their strategy was focused strictly on coping. When Phil, our friend Chip and I went to interview the therapists at the rehab center, everyone was nice but they spoke to Phil as if he were slightly deaf or from a foreign country. An exaggerated smile went with the extra volume and the slow, carefully-enunciated words, "Grab the handle right here." We walked out of the facility, looked at each other and said the same thing.

"We can do better than this."

And we did.

Friends provided the expertise and resources to help develop an independent program. Chip, a lifelong fitness expert, set up a weight-lifting program designed to rebuild the strength in Phil's large muscles. The theory was that, like a baby, it is not possible to have fine motor control without gross motor control. This idea made sense to me. You can't shave your face unless your arm is strong enough to hold the razor.

Right!

Phil enjoyed working out, but he hated therapy.

"Why do therapy when I can do a workout?"

The new rehab program was a modified Olympic workout—two sessions a week using regular gym equipment, in a garage.

Great!

Phil started by doing 1/4 squats off the couch with Chip helping him up. By the third month, he was doing blaster squats with a hundred pounds. The amazing results could be seen in body *and* mind. After the squat workout, Phil's brain would suddenly explode with energy and his original thinking lasted all day. The disappointment was that the burst of mental improvement would slip into fatigue and confusion the next day.

Exhaustion was the aftermath of these workouts, and massage was one way we improved his recovery time. He gave every ounce of effort to the workouts, but then would be unable to move, speak or hold up his head.

Overcoming fatigue became the driving factor in life. All mental and physical function was impacted—mood, coordination, muscle function, mental function. The brain injury seemed to have a fatigue cycle of its own. We couldn't tell which days Phil would feel okay or too tired to move. He would often experience complete central nervous system exhaustion, so flexibility ruled.

After a month of workouts, Phil started moving a bit better. Two months later he could get up out of a chair without help. Four mon73, ths later he could get in and out of the car alone. Six months later he was throwing away his cane.

Whenever Phil improved enough to get rid of a piece of equipment, we took it right over to hospice. Neither of us wanted to keep the stuff around a minute longer than we had to.

Sleep deprivation continued to be a problem. Phil worried that I would be killed or never return every time I left him.

Exhaustion sapped his optimism. The daily battle was to keep him focused on the prize—getting better. He was fighting off daily bouts of afternoon depression. My journal continued to provide the benchmark for progress. It reminded us he was getting better.

Maintaining a positive attitude was critical. We called people we knew every time something good happened. Sharing the excitement kept us excited.

Friends helped. Exercise helped. Naps helped. Marking progress helped.

Rehab for the body was just one aspect of Phil's recovery. He needed rehab for everything. As a lifelong reader, he was crushed when he tried to read and couldn't go from sentence to sentence.

There were several problems. His eyes no longer worked in tandem. His short-term memory was so short that he couldn't remember the first half of the sentence by the time he got to the second half. His anger fuse was less than half a second long. Consequently, each time he tried to read anything, the effort would end in cursing and books or magazines flying across the room.

In stepped Chip and Robert Service. Chip bought us a book of the collected works of the poet Robert Service. Service is one of the famous trench poets from World War I, known by many as the Bard of the Yukon. He wrote about the war but is more famous for "The Shooting of Dan McGrew" and "The Cremation of Sam McGee" as well as other tales from the gold rush. They are all manly poems that meant to be read aloud.

There are strange things done in the midnight sun
By the men who moil for gold;
The Arctic trails have their secret tales
That would make your blood run cold...

Robert Service became a part of our morning schedule. Phil read three poems aloud each morning. He struggled with the words and pronunciations. He was difficult to understand. He cursed and shouted and yelled. But he didn't give up. Every day he read aloud and every day he got better. At the end of the year, Phil could read again. Slowly, carefully, with notations in the margins to keep track of characters and ideas, he could read.

Phil's progress became the focal point of our existence. And with each improvement, life started getting easier. The hospitals got him started, but home is where he got better.

Television was extremely difficult for Phil to follow. The violence was too much—even the national news was overwhelming. Fortunately, we had our local news that came with a lot of laughs. The weather girl had a habit of making a tiny cough and then saying, "Excuse me." Phil nicknamed her Erin "Excuse Me" Brown and we made bets every night on how many *excuse me's* Erin could get into her two-minute segment.

The only other programs that were watchable were all nature shows narrated by Peter Coyote. We learned about sled dogs and lions. We laughed about slug love.

Every day Phil worked hard pushing the edges of raging anger and then we would laugh. We laughed a lot every single day.

Chapter 11
Get Smart

Living with a brain injury has been far from easy because my physical and emotional limitations kept making it harder for each other to recover. Of course, the body and mind are a single organism. I've only separated them for clarity, not reality.

BUILDING A SMARTER MIND

My healing process would have taken forever if I hadn't changed my mental attitude in the following ways:

I had to get angry about my limitations.

I had to stop blaming myself.

I had to accept that my new behavior was not my fault and put that energy into recovering.

I had to realize that my fears seemed scarier than they really were.

I had to make taking mild anti-depressants a daily reality. It took me years before I'd even consider taking one and when I finally did, I wondered why I'd waited so long.

I had to fight depression by sticking to a firm schedule. Knowing what's next was uplifting and not knowing was often depressing and confusing.

I had to fight depression by staying busy. This left no time to mope.

I had to quit worrying about being confused. I had to keep reminding myself that everybody else is too.

I had to stick to regular aerobic activity. This may sound like something that was only good for my body, but it also made my mind twice as efficient.

I had to stop worrying about getting lost. As it turned out, worrying about getting lost was more trouble than being lost.

I had to write everything down. Having things on paper took them out of my mind, reminded me and made me calmer immediately.

I had to realize that being alone not only got easier, it was more fun.

Since the new me needed a more regular schedule and my memory wasn't what it used to be, it paid to write one down and follow it. Here's how it looked:

Sunday A.M.	2 hours relaxing in the sun and reading
Sunday P.M.	Lunch, nap, TV news shows, more reading, more resting, dinner, TV movie, crash at 9:00
Monday A.M.	Focused writing
Monday P.M.	Heavy leg day in the gym, reading, lunch, nap, more resting, TV-movie, crash at 9:00
Tuesday A.M.	Focused writing
Tuesday P.M.	Core day in the gym. Repeat Monday PM
Wednesday A.M.	Focused writing
Wednesday P.M.	Upper body routine in gym. Repeat Monday P.M.

And so it went until six tightly scheduled days brought me back to Sunday again. I found I needed at least one day off a week. And it seemed best to do the hardest stuff, like writing, in the morning and save the physical stuff for the afternoon. That counterpoint was very efficient because they made each other more effective.

The following realizations have worked so well for me, I've come to think of them as sound advice.

Get Daily Booster Shots
Say, "GOOD!" out loud. Say it often.

High-five yourself in the mirror.

Give yourself frequent cheers. Do this whenever you make progress, get something done or achieve any goal. You don't need a hysterical crowd, hundreds of hand-held cards that say GO BEARS! or a big brass band. Just yell, "Right on!" or "Way to go!" or "Nice job!" and yell it out LOUD.

Do something uplifting whenever you're down. This could be listening to your favorite Gypsy Kings album, reading a Robert Crais mystery or drinking a glass of your favorite wine.

Personally, I've given up classical music and medieval scholarship, but you should stick with them as long as they make your day. If you can't find any dusty medieval tomes to read, just do a friend a favor.

Enjoy Mini-Victories
Small things count, like finding a lost pen under the car seat, learning the quickest way to fold laundry or finding the exact tool for the job.

Avoid Big Surprises
Strangely, this includes pleasant surprises too. Believe it or not, they cost the same amount of energy as unpleasant surprises. Having a friend drop by to say hello is as much work as dropping a glass on the kitchen floor.

And, of course, this includes any sudden loud noises.

BANG!

See?

By the way, I still jump when a car backfires or the wind slams a door.

Win the Day

Avoid upsets early in the morning. Stress snowballs, so something that bugs you in the morning can ruin your whole day.

Accept Risk

Carefully selected risky situations are better for your recovery than playing it safe will ever be. Taking risks teaches you how to handle any event with an uncertain outcome. Nothing focuses the mind like a threat to your comfort zone.

Get Used to It

If any of your basic senses were compromised by your brain injury, don't worry about it. Some of them will make a partial comeback, many of them will make a full comeback and some will even improve.

Early on, my sense of smell was so weak I had to put my nose right in the cup to smell the coffee. I still remember the day when I woke up and smelled it brewing from another room.

If any of your senses don't recover, it pays to change your attitude. Forget the fantasy of being perfect and accept the reality of who you are.

And when there's nothing you can do about a situation, you might as well get used to it.

Dump Bad Habits

If you've gotten sick and tired of being called an obsessive-compulsive or being laughed at for being a sit-com-type perfectionist, it's time to quit that show. I decided it was not okay to be a soap-opera weirdo or a psych case for another day. Is one more day okay with you?

I didn't think so.

So let it be okay to leave the room a little messy. Let misaligned edges stay misaligned. Quit fussing and just leave things where they were. Skip a chore that seems like you have to do it now and do the damn thing later, if at all.

Of course, if you want to keep being a nut job, that's up to you.

Stay Hip

Staying hip counts big time. Nothing's worse for your mind than losing touch with what's happening. Luckily, the Internet, DVDs and TV news shows make staying hip much easier than it ever was. Now you can stay hip right in your own home (and if that sounds like an old ad slogan, I couldn't help myself).

Follow a Regular Schedule

You should try to follow as regular a schedule as possible. A predictable life is calming because it helps avoid ugly disturbances (refer back to my schedule on the previous pages).

Play Memory Games

Invent your own memory drills, like never forgetting anyone's name. At first it may be hard to remember the names of close family and friends. Can you believe I used to forget my own wife's name? But stay with it. You'll get there.

Try the same drill with people you see infrequently, like waiters, shop clerks and landscape workers. I used to have to write their names down, but after a while I began to remember them by heart and so will you.

It seems to me that two names are more memorable than one. I don't know why, but Mary and Phil is easier to remember than either Mary or Phil alone.

It also helps to turn names into memorable phrases. Try adding a word to a name like pool-Mike or plumber-Bill. Make up an imaginary company like Mary of the Mary and Phil Company. Or call someone Gayle with a Y, Tammy with a T, or Phil with a P.

You can play the Birthday Game where you try to remember what you did on past birthdays. Think back to where you were, who was there and the presents you got.

You can try remembering the names of all the car models you know of, or think of failed advertising campaigns, rare flowers or old-time actors.

You can try the one I play every year with my brother. I remember 10 things about our childhood, then give him a quiz on the phone, with questions like the name of our local candy store, the prank we played on Hubba and Robba, or the name of our childhood swim coach.

Improve Your Concentration

Concentration drills are easy to find. Open today's paper and do the Sudoku puzzle or buy one of those large paperbacks that's full of them.

Sudoku involves arranging numbers in a particular set of sequences. In their words, "Sudoku is essentially a game of placing numbers in squares, using very simple rules of logic and deduction." This sounds easy, but it can actually be a tortuous exercise, especially with a brain injury. At first you may not be able to complete the puzzle at all. However, if you time yourself every day, you'll find you'll get faster in a week.

There are also professional methods of building concentration like biofeedback for the brain. It does require a qualified person to provide the equipment and the expertise, but it's a simple process. Several points on the outside of your head are wired to a computer screen. Then, you just sit in there and play computer games. The idea is to move a graphic like Pac Man through a maze at faster and faster speeds, or to steer a sailboat between two points. Believe it or not, but you can actually make computer graphics move with your brain alone.

Take a Break

Breaks are good. Whenever I'm writing, I use three different stretch sessions as breaks to keep me fresh. Kind of a triple that clears my mind, boosts my energy and loosens my body for the rest of the day.

That reminds me. I'll be back in a minute.

Reading Skills

Reading after the crash was torturous at first. I couldn't read two sentences before forgetting what had happened the two sentences before that. I couldn't remember who the characters were and what was going on from one chapter to the next. I used to underline character names or write them all down with descriptions and relevant details.

After years of working my way from paragraphs to pages and pages to books, I finally passed my reading test.

These days I can finally enjoy reading for about an hour a day. I do this by creating a ladder of reading goals and creating accomplishments that anybody can follow.

An easy way to start is simply by trying to read more sentences, paragraphs and pages than you did last time. Then try to read for longer and longer sessions. Then work your way up to a book a week or a book a month.

One day you'll be able to remember the plot twists and character names in a novel by heart.

Knightly. His name is Knightly.

Plan Ahead

Make dealing with natural disasters as smooth as possible by having a ready-bag that's always ready. It should have a change of clothes, underwear, medication, an extra pair of glasses, a radio, a decent book, a sweat suit, a working flashlight, a first aid kit and there should always be gas in your car.

In 2006, the Island of Hawaii experienced a magnitude 6.7 earthquake that terrified me. Knowing that I had my kit made me feel safer.

Make Socializing Work Harder

Start thinking of friendly chats as practice sessions with goals, instead of small talk to pass the time. It helps to think of them as Chat Drills.

Think about the time you spend with friends as a training opportunity when you train yourself to act normally. A cup of coffee with friends at Starbucks is more than a break—it's an opportunity to work on being good company.

Prepare topics of conversation that have nothing to do with you and your TBI trauma. Like current politics, world events, how to make the best pizza dough, an interesting idea about evolution, anything but your last doctor's appointment.

See how long you can stay focused on a conversation, then stay focused longer the next time.

Practice being good company by being interesting, interactive and funny.

Try to make accurate facial expressions and use graceful body language.

Fun and Funny

Being funny is a good goal. Being a good comic is a natural talent, but you should try to be as amusing as you can and monitor your friend's responses. You can do this by memorizing shaggy dog stories or other funny stories and telling them better every time. Even better, write your own.

A great example of this is the Aristocrats. The Aristocrats is a famous long joke that comedians love because so much of it is delivered impromptu. Comics actually write the off-the-cuff details as they give them. It pays to learn it and write your own details as you tell it.

Mental Games
It's great to make up your own mental games, games that are especially compelling to you. Are you a birder? A football fan? A connoisseur of single malt Scotch? A lover of impressionist art? Just pick the subject you find most interesting and then quiz yourself on the right details.

My personal favorite is designing my perfect house. Even though I'm no architect, I enjoy the problem-solution process. Who knows—my rough sketches may come in handy some day!

Car and Driver
Riding shotgun took a long time to get used to, but driving was a whole other ballgame. Here's what I finally learned:

Practicing on deserted roads gives you time to get used to driving again.

Turning off the radio and getting rid of distractions makes it easier.

Small cars are easier to handle.

Lower speeds are both safer and easier. Your brain simply doesn't work as fast as it used to.

Take straight roads whenever you can. This isn't always possible but it helps.

BUILDING A SMARTER BODY
Take Daily Naps
Having an injured brain calls for a new way to think about your body. Used correctly, a smart body can help your brain send better signals.

For starters, daily naps are a must since injured brains need more than the normal amount of rest. Getting a few hours of sleep may work for students during finals, soldiers on a mission or jet-lagged executives, but a short doze just isn't enough for you. No, you simply have to accept the fact that rest doesn't accumulate like it used to. A good night's sleep only lasts for a day. A nap only lasts for the rest of the afternoon and your rest bank is always overdrawn.

Even though naps are never as restful as a whole night's sleep, they will help you stay alert through the afternoon and evening. Crashing for a half hour after lunch may not make you feel like a new day has dawned, but it will keep you awake until 9:00 or 10:00 at night. I take one every day at one o'clock because it's the only way I can stay awake that late.

Dump Those Aids

The sooner you start dumping your aids, the better. Nothing feels as good as dumping a wheelchair for a walker, dumping a walker for a cane or dumping a cane and walking without one.

Sit Down and Shut Up

Sitting down means the brain doesn't have to make the millions of cell connections it needs to stand up. Shutting up means it doesn't have to use the millions of connections it needs to be witty, clever or polite.

Sitting down and shutting up does a lot more than rest your vocal chords and feet. It's the fastest way I know to get rebooted.

Eat Slowly

TBIs often compromise the swallowing and sinus functions. If your injury has left you with this problem, you already know that eating too quickly can cause a choking fit. This is not only embarrassing—it's dangerous.

Unfortunately, coughing causes more coughing. Coughing jags start a chain reaction that cause a runny nose, which causes more coughing, which causes a runny nose, which causes even more coughing, and so on. Around it goes until you've got an out-of-control coughing jag. Now all eyes are on you and people are offering everything from sorrowful looks to glasses of water to wads of Kleenex. Not okay!

You just can't eat as quickly or be as careless about it as you used to be. So don't. Since family dinners, anniversaries and lunches with friends can't be avoided, it pays to follow your mother's advice:

Slow down and chew your food. You'll enjoy it more if you don't talk with your mouth full.

I'd like to add this as well: Separate meals and visits if you can, talk between swallows if you can't. Just nod the rest of the time. It's good to practice multi-tasking, but not at the table.

If you'd like to give up some meals altogether, the marketplace can help. These days, health food and fitness stores are crammed with all kinds of tasty energy bars and nutritional drinks. There's a whole array from protein drinks to delicious carbo drinks in every flavor. Many even have complete doses of daily vitamins and minerals. If you slug one of these down before you visit someone, you can say you're just not hungry when you get there.

Do Eye Exercises
Eye muscles work like any other muscles in your body. They get more tired as the day goes on. Like other muscles, they respond to training. There are a number of eye routines that improve your ability to focus, strengthen your peripheral vision and build visual endurance in general. It pays to find them and do them.

I do exercises from the Feldenkreis system, but there are others that work just as well.

Try, Try Again

Trying has helped me deal with dozens of limitations. Trying got me from one to three mile markers on the road, from one lap to a kilometer in the pool. Trying got me more reps and heavier weights in the gym. And trying has just gotten me to the end of this chapter.

Chapter 12
Smart Therapy

Even though I knew my head injury was biological, depression and thoughts about suicide were happening way too often. It was happening so frequently that I knew I'd better try some psychological therapy.

Discussing psychological therapy is a tough one for me, because I've always been conflicted about it. On the one hand, as an action-oriented guy I'm against it in principle. On the other hand, behavioral therapy did help me forestall thoughts about suicide.

Anyway, the conflict-kid will now try to be objective so you can make your own decision.

THE PROS

If you can find a well-respected behaviorist (or cognitive therapist) who's up on the latest techniques, make a short-term arrangement with an end-game in sight. A good behaviorist can help you understand the basics of a TBI and recommend the best new attitudes that will help you overcome your worrisome new challenges.

Neither of us should ever forget that the new us needs a new type of cognitive therapy.

I hired Doctor Mary Hibbard back in my early days. She was six thousand miles away in New York, so we had to settle for phone therapy. We were only face-to-face once, but she became a friend who gave me a lot of useful advice about dealing with my TBI. She helped me understand the demands that come from living with a smaller brain and what my new goals should be going forward.

Her advice only works if you remember two important points: one, you should ignore the medical averages because you're not average. And two, even the most respected averages are directional at best.

Good behaviorists will reassure you by letting you know just how common fatigue and depression are. They will help you understand that your new limitations are only as real as you make them. They will coach you through dealing with your convenient lies, and they will help you develop a set of more realistic expectations.

They will also help you understand the eccentricities behind your symptoms. Things like talking to yourself out loud, getting angry about nothing and irrational feelings like thinking you're being punished for something. Not to mention frequent forgetfulness, the unexplained obsession to count everything, your need to create rigid rules, your insistence on being exact and your uncontrollable rigidity.

You may even come to accept that your eccentricities don't make you a weirdo. You're no weirder than anybody else and these are just common TBI symptoms.

If your brain injury is less than 10 years old, someone like Dr. Hibbard can save you a lot of time, energy and embarrassment. After all, you've got a new bike and you need an instruction manual to put it together.

Lastly and most importantly, a good behaviorist can help you manage your fatigue by teaching you how it brings on states of depression, anger, confusion and annoying perseveration. What's perseveration? The dictionary defines perseveration as *an uncontrollable repetition of a particular response despite the absence of stimulus; usually caused by an organic disorder.*

My own definition is much simpler. When you perseverate, your mind is stuck trying to solve a totally unimportant problem that's already been solved. You're stuck as you try to remember the names of irrelevant people, places, products, book and movie titles. You might be stuck listing meaningless details.

The best behaviorists can tell you that a good way to break free from this annoying, pain-in-the-ass process is to get more rest than you did before you were grabbed by the TBI monster. Behaviorism gives you the understanding it takes to live with the new you and deal with your new obstacles.

One highly controversial technique I tried after my crash is worth mentioning because it was so effective. It's called Eye Movement, Desensitization and Reprocessing (or EMDR). In textbook language, "EMDR is an integrative psychotherapy approach. It involves dual stimulation using verbal statements and bilateral eye movements or taps on the knee."

EMDR is the primary treatment for post-traumatic stress syndrome, which I had in spades. I was nervous about driving too fast, passing big trucks or being followed too closely. In fact, driving of any kind caused my heart to race.

My EMDR sessions would begin with me telling about the trauma I had been through. Then I would rate it on a "upset" scale from one to five. The doctor would tap on my knees while I repeated what I had just said.

Then I would rate those experiences on the trauma scale again.

Eureka!

After just a few minutes of simultaneous talking and tapping, my trauma score would drop dramatically (a score of five would become a score of two, and so on). This new lower score would tell us both that total relearning had taken place and that my trauma didn't bother me as much as it did.

How does this all this work?

When a person goes through a big crisis, the memory of the crisis is stored in the body as well as in the brain. A common symptom of brain injuries is that these two departments don't work together, so it's necessary to awaken both parts in order for them to work simultaneously. Thus bodily sensations (knee tapping) have to accompany talking about the subject.

For me, my body was still hanging on to some worrisome emotions about the crash long after it happened. This resulted in both psychological tension and tight muscles. When the above relearning took place, the traumatic experience moved out of my body and was allowed to relocate in my verbal memory so it could be resolved by discussion. EMDR resolved my traumatic memories by dumping the tension held in my brain and allowing my body to shed its own stressful memories. Thus, the ugly feelings associated with the crash became far less bothersome.

My session was considered successful because I could remember the crash without getting pain from tight muscles.

EMDR experts believe that positive self-beliefs are important, but they have to be believed by the body as well. EMDR worked for me big time. After just four sessions, I had numerous insights and a valuable relearning process, and I felt much better.

But, pal, I hope you'll never forget that no therapy ever substitutes for throwing your leg over the saddle and riding away.

THE CONS

I hope that was a fair rundown of the pros for getting some psychology therapy. Now for the cons. The following people make the case much better than I do:

"The way to get started is to quit talking and begin doing."
WALT DISNEY

"You aren't learning anything when you're talking."
LYNDON B. JOHNSON

"Intention without action is useless."
CAROLINE MYSS

"You can stay in therapy your whole life, but you've got to live life and not talk about life."
TRACEY GOLD

And my favorite:

"Life itself remains a very effective therapist."
KAREN HORNEY

But however the big shots say it, when it comes to recovering, walking the walk beats talking the talk every time.

Despite the urgent needs we have in today's combat zones, factories and sports stadiums...despite the advances in emergency care and food chemistry...and despite the progress we've made in hospital technology, brain injuries are still a medical mystery.

Even if we include the dramatic advances made in ongoing care, there are very few therapists who know more than the simple basics about a TBI, especially the more traditional therapists. Most of them are burdened down with baggage from an earlier age, like the tired principles from Psychology 101 or the cold leftovers from Freudian recipes.

You may be stuck with a therapist whose goals don't suit you at all (like overcoming a new challenge every day). Maybe you've tried the challenge-a-day strategy for a while and run out of new ones. Maybe what's left seems like a waste of time or maybe you'd feel better attacking your own list of challenges.

After a year of phone sessions with Dr. Hibbard, I found that many of her suggestions were not good for me or just impossible. She kept urging me to be out and about all day long. She recommended that I get an easy, full-time job like flipping burgers or a more challenging full-time job at the Hawaii Tourism Bureau. On top of that, writing was discouraged as too difficult a field for TBI victims. She told me, "Writing isn't social enough and it can be very upsetting."

That may be true, but whether writing is an upsetting field or not, every brain injury has different effects. *The important thing is trying to get better at what's important to you.* As the big shots said earlier, trying isn't about talking, it's about taking action.

There are hundreds of happy examples of people who have won by taking action after great personal traumas. There are even many notable brain injury victims who beat the odds by trying hard and succeeding big time. If you can return to teaching, the military, the fire department, a restaurant, a mining crew, a real estate office, the police department, or any other career—DO IT. If you're fortunate enough to be artistic, dramatic, athletic or performance-oriented in any way, get back to it—the world needs you.

I was lucky. I'm a committed writer and writing is a solo job. Originally, I experienced serious memory loss, daily confusion and too much computer anger.

But since writing has always been a passion, I overcame fatigue by writing in the morning. I overcame confusion with planning. And I managed my computer anger by endlessly fiddling with the damn thing. *Gnilddif wiht nmad gniht!*

If you're like most people, you have a passion of some kind. If it's down in the basement, bring it up and give it some fresh air. If it's up in the dusty attic, bring it down and shake it out.

If your passion is as physical as hunting, fishing or running—clean that rifle, oil that fly reel or buy some new running shoes. If it's as static as cards, chess, or checkers—join a bridge club, read about the master's strategies or yell, "AHA!" as you triple jump over your friend's unlucky pieces.

If you're passionate about your work, you're a lucky guy. If you don't think you have a passion and you've already looked in the cellar and the attic, it's probably out in the garden shed.

Once you've found it, joy will help you keep it. But never talk it to death. Talk therapy spends the vital energy you need now, more than ever. The last thing you need is a weekly mope.

Writing has always been my passion and no psychologist was going to rule it out. Thanks to the right drugs, I was able to say goodbye to yammering to anybody but myself.

BEFORE

BEFORE

DURING

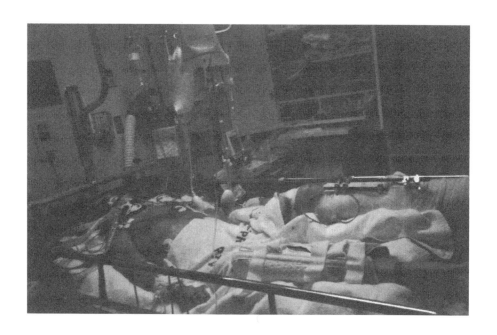

DURING

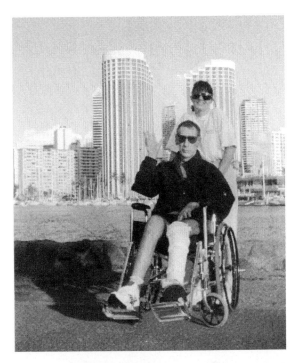

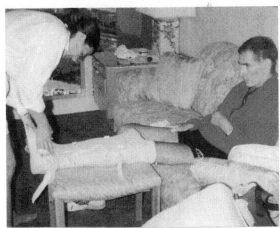

AFTER

AFTER

NOW

Chapter 13
Smart Drugs

Today's medical professionals know that many drug treatments for brain damage have proven to be very successful. They know that the brain is just like any other muscle and should be treated like any other broken part of the body.

Personally, I think drugs are both faster and more direct, not to mention saving years of psychological therapy.

Now I can say hello to a whole group of effective new brain drugs and goodbye to annoying therapy appointments. Hello to Zoloft and goodbye to those expensive yakity-yak sessions. Hello to Ritalin and goodbye to those unwanted personal questions. Hello to Aricept and goodbye to those embarrassing invasions.

All these new drugs, and many others, have set me free from foolish talk and questionable advice, and they do it in a fraction of the time. Any honest behavioral therapist will admit this and recommend the right medication even if it means losing the patient. After all, when it comes to behavior-modification, the brain only knows when things are okay and it doesn't care why.

It should be said, however, that today's brain drugs work well *as long as they're the right ones in the right dosages*. Taking too high a dose of the right drug is the same mistake as taking the wrong drug.

Too high a high dose of Adderall, for instance, made me anxious, disagreeable and dizzy right away. Too low a dose of anything is ineffective.

When it comes to drugs like Zoloft, Aricept, Ritalin, Pamelor or Adderall, neither the manufacturer's brochures or the Physicians' Desk Reference (PDR) gave fine enough readings to customize the right dose for me. Their general calculations are based on severity charts, age, height and weight, and not much else.

It took me several years of annoying trial and error to get it right. These days I take light doses of Zoloft and infrequent doses of Ritalin.

Whether you end up taking light, infrequent or half doses, there's still no way to believe that you're drug-dependent forever, is there?

I couldn't believe it either. I was always quitting and once or twice I even flushed some damn prescription down the john.

Drug dependent forever? No way!

Sounds familiar, doesn't it? As hard as it is to accept being drug-dependent, you need to accept it, just like you had to accept your new limitations.

One more time:

As hard as it is to accept being drug-dependent, you need to accept it, just like you had to accept your new limitations.

It was years before I could admit I was disabled, but it took even more years to admit I was a pill-popper.

Being dependent on drugs is better than being dependent on therapy. I found that today's brain drugs improved life in a very tangible, 3D way. Especially the smart ones.

But even the smartest drugs don't come with a dosage guarantee, so the only sure thing is still trial and error. The right drugs with the right dosage reduced my anxiety level so I could attack life. I could stay on offense and become as independent as possible. And as any coach will tell you, offense beats defense every time.

And even though the wrong dose sizes of the right drugs like Zoloft and Ritalin led to anxiety, I'd do the trial and error process all over again.

Zoloft

Since worry uses up so much valuable energy, it paid to reduce anxiety as much as I could. Zoloft helped with that. As the commercial shows us, it does it by unblocking the route to the happy part of the brain.

This new connection made me less anxious, more mellow and gave me more energy for life. And when my mood and energy levels improved, my performance improved.

Nobody should expect a total bliss-out. Zoloft keeps people from having fewer lows, but no drug can deal with all of life's upsets.

The Zoloft label says it has sexual side effects. Do I have any? None of your business.

Ritalin

Ritalin is prescribed immediately in a lot of TBI cases. It's a completely counter-intuitive drug because it actually stimulates the brain to help it relax.

Really! Stimulating the brain helps it think more clearly, and clearer thinking is more relaxing.

Ritalin does this by creating new pathways around dead brain cells to living ones. These days I not only think more clearly, I feel more confident because I'm a better problem solver. But Ritalin is like a five-hour booster shot, so two doses a day kept me up all day without a nap.

No nap—not okay.

These days I'm down to one 5 mg pill six afternoons a week for the gym. It not only helps me wake up, it makes me want to work out harder. I move more fluidly and it puts me in a better mood when I'm tired. The old me always loved the gym, but Ritalin makes the new me love it all over again.

Energy, mood, performance—all better.

Am I on it as I write this sentence? No way. I don't trust it when it comes to creative decisions. Ritalin gives me too positive an attitude to be editing my own stuff.

One last point. In spite of what I just said about relaxing my mind, Ritalin does nothing to relieve anxiety. I take Zoloft for that and, luckily, the two of them work well together.

Aricept

A relatively new drug called Aricept is terrific—once you get past the dreaded side effects. The dizziness and sore muscles only last a month or so, but you do have to put up with mild stomach upset and a kidney blood test four times a year.

Warnings aside, Aricept is so effective that it gave me the writer's class-A problem: a highly active brain that came with more ideas and the endurance to keep writing.

I started by taking a single 5 mg tablet a day and WOW! It was like a dream come true. New ideas started flowing from first thing in the morning until last thing at night. I was waking up with so many *aha*'s, I actually ran out of Post-It notes.

Sounds great, doesn't it? I thought my prayers were answered until a month later, my highly activated mind got so out of control, I couldn't turn it off. In fact, I was drowning in an idea river 24 hours a day. Sounds like a problem you'd like to have, right? No way. My idea river not only reached flood levels, it created a huge swamp that wouldn't drain all night long. I got nightmares that were impossible to shake off. In fact, they became full-blown hallucinations that lasted after I woke and made me afraid to go to sleep.

Since I didn't want to lose my newly gained writing endurance, I hoped the answer might lie in taking a half dose a day. The good news is that less medication ended the scary nightmares immediately. But the bad news is, less medication didn't help my writing.

Aricept answered my prayers, but the stuff had too high a price. After a month or two, taking half a dose seemed pointless. I decided to quit.

These days, my writing endurance has climbed back to about an hour and a half a day. You'll have to tell me if the idea river is still flowing.

It should be said that Aricept is a helpful medication for many people. It's both a recognized Alzheimer's preventative and a short-term cure. Like Ritalin, Aricept is a brain stimulant that not only speeds up brain signals, it can even improve your general mood. If you end up using it, I hope it works for you.

So you depend on drugs to stay cool and you've finally gotten the dosage right. Good! Now count your blessings and don't mess around anymore. Your brain has a very sensitive and touchy personality. Think of it as an eccentric movie star with a mind of its own. Changes, substitutes, lapses or drug vacations of any kind can upset you so much that they're more trouble than they're worth. Don't do it. Any drug play is foul play.

When it comes to brain damage, we're both dealing with a 3D, photographable reality—dead brain cells. Black holes we ignore at our peril.

Since those black holes were so depressing, I was lucky to find some new role models for inspiration.

Chapter 14
3 BRDS

Mary

"Is that you, Fuzzy?" Phil asked a schnauzer one day. We were walking on the track of Hawaii Preparatory Academy (HPA), a private school in Waimea. Phil asked every schnauzer the same question for years, just in case one of them was his old pal, Fuzzy.

As far as Phil was concerned, the characters of his youth were still alive and well. The names of the shopkeepers in his old New York neighborhood left us snorting. The stories of him and his brother filling the kitchen with soapsuds after seeing Mr. Roberts left us breathless. And the endless Dickinson College stories left us in hysterics.

There was a philosophy professor at Dickinson, Dr. Gould, who lectured about a thinker who was famous for saying, "You just can't know." More snorting. Shoot, Phil even remembered the names of his high school teachers.

These memories from long ago helped keep us going because we were always amused. But the fact that Phil couldn't remember what happened earlier that day was weird.

"I told you we were going to the doctor today."

"Where did you hide the keys?"

"You never told me about that."

All of our friends looked like strangers to him and they were hurt by it. After all, they had just helped us get through the most harrowing experience of our lives. They had reached out and hugged us. They had shared and cared. They had loved us big time. But Phil was unconscious for most of it.

His ability to enjoy people would return. I hoped that over time, Phil would return to the person who enjoyed others. In the meantime, he focused on his physical recovery.

During a typical week, we saw friends every day either at sword training, surfing, the gym or the beach, even at our house for dinner. Those activities weren't very easy anymore, but I knew time and strength would bring them back. Until then, we focused on what Phil could do.

We had to work at getting Phil back to surfing, snowboarding and skateboarding. 3 BRDS, the vanity plate for Phil's black Toyota, helped us do that even though he wasn't the vanity plate type. I just made up my mind that the dusty equipment in the garage wasn't going to stay dusty.

The gym led to more overall strength and coordination and that led us to the HPA track. They have a beautiful track in a dream location. At that time, blooming ironwood trees circled the whole quarter mile.

When we arrived, a light wind-blown mist would be wetting the ground and Phil would get out and start walking. At first, a single loop was a high-five occasion. That effort required 17 months. Later, he was able to do four laps (a mile) in 32 minutes. At that point, he was so determined that he started setting the goal higher and higher. Every week we would have go at the track, but by then Phil was pushing to go faster.

"The proof is on the watch."

The payment was exhaustion for days but we believed the price was worth it. The track gave us a number of goals, but getting to the top of the driveway and back was the first major one on the road to running again.

Going from being a triathlete who could run a 10k in 38 minutes to walking a mile in 32 was a downer for sure.

"I hate my shadow. It goes wherever I go."

"It looks like a cripple's shadow."

"This sucks! When will I be able to run again?"

"If" was never a thought—or, at least, never a spoken one.

Surfing was the other activity that Phil couldn't let go. Before the accident, he hooted and hollered every time he caught a wave. He just LOVED it! But getting back to it was a daunting obstacle. Just the task of walking across the sand kept him out of the ocean for almost a year. It was 16 months before he could walk across the beach without help.

The big flat surfboard was back in action. He would slide on it and try to paddle along the beach. Since he only had one arm that worked, he kept making counter-clockwise circles. Going in a circle was only one of his problems. The other was balance.

Staying prone on the board was a challenge, but getting back on after tipping over was an even bigger one. The amazing thing was that he was like one of those wind-up birds that just kept pecking the water and getting back up. Over and over and over.

Sometimes, Phil would sit up and ride it over the swells like a bucking bronco. Then he would eggbeater it around with his legs and look at me every time he made a 360.

The lap pool at the Mauna Lani Racquet Club was our favorite swimming spot. After the accident, we met a cute bouncy blonde with a muscular back who happened to be an incredible swimmer and an inspiring instructor. Shannon Heringer met us once a week at the pool and worked with Phil to reclaim his swimming skills.

In time, Phil was able to do laps again, but they were a big come-down for him. He slogged them out with sinking legs, a cramped left arm and an unresponsive left leg. But he did them. Lap after painful lap.

The ocean wasn't doable if Phil couldn't swim well enough to save himself. That meant he was stuck in the pool.

"So what?"

Phil's snowboard was still hanging in the garage. Now that he could walk, maybe he could catch a few runs on the slopes. All that was missing was restoring his balance.

The Perform Better catalog had foam rollers that could be used to do just that. They also had a cool skateboard-sized balance board that could be the next step. We bought all this stuff and started working on it.

It turns out that balance is a complicated activity.

First, you need to feel your feet and have a sense of what's happening down there. The damage to Phil's left foot left him without any sensation in it. It's not easy to balance on a left foot that isn't sending any signals.

Second, the leg and hip muscles need to be strong and flexible enough to adjust to the signals from the feet. Phil's legs were still a mess. Both knees had torn ligaments and a serious dislocation, so they were very unstable. His upper left femur had suffered a compound fracture and the hip and leg were still very stiff. His lower left leg sustained multiple compound fractures and significant tissue loss. The doctors had to reroute his soleus muscle from the back of the leg to cover the giant hole along the front of the leg. Compounding the problem, the orthopedic surgeon reset the bone so it was straight when you looked at it from the front but the piece closest to the ankle was canted to the rear.

Third, balance is tied to the inner ear and the brain's processing mechanism. Phil had trouble with dizziness and light nausea every time he sat up, stood up or turned his head too fast.

Fourth, the eyes are required to keep your visual field steady and Phil's eyes weren't working together at all. One looked one to the right all the time and the other was able to follow the action.

With all these problems, standing on a balance board was harder than an act at the Big Top.

Through it all, Phil's anger was a great motivator. He yelled obscenities that would make your grandmother blush. He threw objects around the room. He sweated bullets. But he didn't give up.

What could we do to give him some board love? After conferences with our friends, we thought the snowboard might be the easiest of the three sports to make happen. Snowboarding required that both feet be tied into the board so it's really a full-body movement. No problem, Phil could move his whole body very well. Falling might be a problem but we could 'walk' him down the slope from person to person and help him get up after falls.

Of course the biggest advantage of snowboarding is that the ground is stable. Unlike surfing where the ocean is always moving.

Chip had relocated to Sedona and was near the Brian Head Ski Resort. He agreed to meet us in Utah to help out.

The ride over on the airplane was frightening. Phil was lost and confused. Going to the restroom meant walking down the aisle and that required serious balance. The people, the noise and the chaos of the airport kept Phil anxious and angry. The distances he had to walk were vast and Phil would not get in a wheelchair.

Landing in Vegas was okay. It was warm enough and the break gave us a chance to shut out the world and rest. We did a night on the ground and then we drove north to the ski resort. As we drove into Utah's mountains, the snow made an appearance. By the time we got to Brian Head, ice and snow were everywhere. Phil was anxious about getting there so I kept driving.

Snowboarding? Are we crazy?

At the condo, the problems became apparent. The parking lot and sidewalk were caked in a thick coating of irregular ice. Phil slipped around it with a deer-in-the-headlights look.

Chip arrived with his son and we made a plan.

First, we took a couple of days of rest. Easy access was critical so we scouted around looking for a gently graded slope. We had to reach both the top and bottom by car.

The cold kept Phil shivering, no matter how many sweaters, shirts and hats he wore. He stayed in the condo a lot, resting. We brought in food and he rested some more.

Then the day arrived. It was now or never.

Phil put on his snowboarding stuff. He added wrist guards, knee and elbow pads. With one of us on either side, he struggled to the top of the slope.

"Don't help me, I got it."

Sitting in the snow and attaching his feet to the board required a Herculean effort. Not to mention getting up again—Chip needed to help him. Finally Phil was up, fully costumed in shredder attire. Excited. Terrified. Embarrassed. He stood there for what seemed a long, long time.

When he was ready for a run, Chip helped him get started. He did it! I caught him and helped get down the next few feet. Back to Chip, back to me, back to Chip.

"No more help!" he yelled and the last few feet were his alone. A triumph!

Then came the struggle back to the car, the loading of the equipment, another two days of rest and then back to Vegas for the confusing flight home.

At the end of the day, we had a sad realization. The cold, the ice, the fragility of Phil's knees, the difficulty of balance were all clear to us now. We knew that this was probably the last snowboard ride Phil would have in his life.

Snowboarding was gone forever. A memory never to be repeated.

With one board down, it was back to surfing.

We couldn't help wondering how Phil would ever "get up and riding" again. So, sitting on the Mauna Kea beach one day, we decided to start on a sponge board.

"No sponge boards, please! Let's get a boogie board."

Phil thought that boogie boards were not only more serious, they had fins so were easier to maneuver. He could push himself off the bottom of the ocean into a tiny breaking wave and feel the joy again. That was all he wanted.

Shannon and I were willing helpers. The three of us walked out together holding hands and dragging the board through the shallow water out to the little break.

When the moment arrived, we shoved off and Phil caught a wave.

Hoots and hollers. Laughter. High-fives. Success!

Phil tried another. And another. And another. Then a slightly larger wave came and Phil tried again. He wasn't able to shift his weight back quickly enough and he endoed, flipping over the front of the board and landing on his head. We pulled him up and his neck was killing him. He could barely hold his head up. We yelled for the lifeguards. They put him on the stretcher and stabilized his neck. Then it was on to the emergency room in Waimea.

Triumph quickly turned to disaster. Now there was real fear. Had he broken his neck?

X-rays. Waiting. Pain.

Finally, a conclusion. No broken neck, just strained neck muscles.

After six months of strained neck muscles, the cost of injury became apparent. No walking. No gym. No swimming. He was in extreme discomfort sitting, lying, even standing. Rehabilitation again. Misery again. Embarrassment again.

Two boards down.

Phil made up his mind to get back to running, swimming and "gymming." We decided to walk along the beach as part of our routine. Walking in sand is great for increasing strength and agility. We had lots of sand, so walking up and down the beach became part of our weekly activities. Then we thought, maybe Phil could walk farther if he wasn't carrying all of his weight. If he walked in the ocean at about waist-high water, it would provide resistance and still be easier to move. That was the theory.

Unfortunately, everything came back to balance. One day walking in the ocean, a small surge came in just as Phil was walking over some irregular sand. His left foot landed crooked because he couldn't shift his weight fast enough. He landed with his toes straight. One toe bent backward and broke.

Lifeguards again. Stabilize again. Embarrassment again. Up to the emergency room. It was really broken so we headed to Oahu to see a podiatrist who pinned the bones. Now Phil had a pin sticking out of his toe for two months.

Back to the pain, the discomfort, the difficulty of lying, sitting and standing. Rehabilitation again. Misery again.

Years were passing and we no longer wanted to keep repeating these mistakes that took months and months to heal. We knew now that Phil's last board—skateboarding—was out. Through it all he still held out for the possibility that he might be able to skateboard again, but at last the sad realization hit home.

No more 3 BRDS.

Phil had to leave the old Phil behind and embrace the new Phil. We needed to take a step back, slow down and be more sensitive to his new body, his new mind and his new realities.

Chapter 15
New Role Models

I was very depressed by the black holes on my x-rays, so I needed a booster shot of heroic inspiration right away. My old role models weren't working anymore so the new me just had to find some new ones.

Scott O'Grady

I started defining my new role models by comparing them with my old role models.

Scott O'Grady is a great example of a previous hero because his escape and evasion story has become a legend. He's the classic school-boy hero who used his ingenuity in combat to overcome almost impossible odds.

Scott is well-known as the US pilot who was shot down over Bosnia and lived to tell about it. After digging a hole and camouflaging himself in it, he survived for five days by eating bugs and drinking rainwater. Security procedures prevented him from using his radio and all he saw were enemy feet and cow hooves.

Scott was important to me because I used to say, "If he can live on bugs and drink rainwater for five days, I can fight off depression in Hawaii."

But Scott has become less of a role model these days because I've come to understand that overcoming obstacles was his only choice.

My newer role models are people who *did* have a choice. They've changed from studs like Scott O'Grady to people who have to deal with personal limitations every day. Remember earlier when I talked about Ganesha, the Hindu god who is revered for removing obstacles? Laura Hillenbrand, Lance Armstrong, Bethany Hamilton and Charles Krauthammer have become Ganesha-heroes to me because they have denied their disabilities and overcome huge obstacles to pursue their life-long passions. In fact, because of them denial has become my best friend.

Laura Hillenbrand

Laura was diagnosed with chronic fatigue syndrome in 1974 at the age of 19. After spending years in bed, she improved enough to find a way to integrate two of her passions—riding horses and writing books. She did this by writing the best-selling novel, *Seabiscuit*, which was also made into a movie.

As a life-long horsewoman, Laura had this big idea as she watched the 1988 Kentucky Derby. She immediately began working on her novel and the rest is literary history.

Even though she suffers from vertigo and is largely housebound, a few years ago she finished her second book called *Unbroken*, another true story about physical heroism. It quickly became her second best-seller in 2010.

Laura has moved into first place on my role model list because we have something very important in common: on-going fatigue. And before Laura, it was Lance Armstrong.

Lance Armstrong

At 25, everybody wondered if Lance Armstrong was the world's best cyclist. He answered that question by winning several World

Championships like The Tour Du Pont and multiple stages of the Tour de France.

In 1996 he was diagnosed with testicular cancer. His tumor then metastasized to his brain and lungs. His treatments included brain and testicular surgery as well as extensive chemotherapy. Lance's prognosis was originally poor, but he has done far more than just survive.

Lance won the Tour de France a record-breaking seven years in a row, between 1999 and 2005. He is the only person to have done this, having broken the previous record of five wins. He only came in third in 2009, but Lance has proved that he's not one to give up. Even despite the controversy surrounding the use of performance-enhancing drugs in this grueling competitive sport, there's no question that Lance has pushed past his limitations to achieve incredible success.

Go Lance!

Bethany Hamilton

Thirteen-year-old surfer Bethany Hamilton was attacked by a shark in 2003. But losing her left arm and almost losing her life hasn't stopped her at all. By age 19, Bethany was back catching big waves on a specially designed surfboard, and she's written a book about her journey back to the water.

"I'm there to have fun and not be scared because it is pretty rare for someone to get attacked twice," she told CNN in late 2004. "The day I got back on my board...it was not necessarily hard. I was just so glad to get back in the water, because I'd been anxious for like a week. When I first got up on my first wave, or it was actually my third wave, but I rode it all the way to the beach, and after that, I just had, like, tears of happiness...I was so stoked to be out there."

That same year Bethany placed fifth in the National Surfing Championships and secured a spot on the US National Surfing Team. She also won an ESPY award from ESPN for Best Comeback athlete and a special courage award at the 2004 Teen Choice Awards.

Bethany's experiences compelled her to write the book, *Soul Surfer,* which made the Los Angeles Times best-seller list and was made into a movie.

What happened to Bethany, happened to me. For her it was a shark, for me it was a drunk driver. We both need all the resilience and hope we can get.

Charles Krauthammer

At age 63, Charles Krauthammer is a retired psychiatrist, a syndicated columnist and a widely respected political commentator.

When he was 22 years old and in medical school, he dove off a diving board and broke his neck. But that didn't hold him back. Even though he was confined to a wheelchair for life, Krauthammer went on to complete his medical degree, become a psychiatrist and pursue his passion for public policy in Washington.

He became an editor on both *The Weekly Standard* and *The New Republic,* as well as a regular panelist on Fox's Special Report and their show, "Inside Washington." His weekly column appears in *The Washington Post* and is syndicated in more than 200 newspapers and media outlets. Charles also became a prominent speech writer and began writing back page essays for *Time Magazine.*

Krauthammer is physically limited and suffers from chronic pain, but he has managed to become a major public persona in spite of it. He is out there every day—on the news, at speaking engagements and at social events. If you only saw him on television, you would never know he is disabled because he keeps his disability to himself and beats the odds on such a grand scale. I believe Krauthammer is one of the best extemporaneous speakers I've ever seen.

Whenever I'm feeling embarrassed or worried about what others might think of me, I remember Charles Krauthammer and just move on.

Erik Weihenmayer

As Time Magazine reported in 2001, Erik Weihenmayer is the first blind person to reach the summit of Mount Everest. Erik also completed the Seven Summits in 2002 and is the author of *Touch the Top of the World: A Blind Man's Journey to Climb Farther Than the Eye Can See.*

Erik is also an acrobatic skydiver, long distance biker, marathon runner, skier, ice climber, hiker and rock climber. He is a friend of Sabriye Tenberken and Paul Kronenberg, the co-founders of Braille Without Borders, whom he visited in Tibet where he climbed with members of the school for the blind.

Erik simply doesn't let his blindness keep him from his dreams.

Marla Runyan

Marla is the first legally blind track athlete to compete in the Olympic Games. She went from being a heptathelete in 1996 to becoming a 1,500-meter Olympic runner and to being ranked No. 1 in the US in the 5 km and marathon runs in 2002. She finished as the top American in the 2002 New York Marathon and set the second-fastest time ever by a US woman at two hours and 27 minutes.

Marla has earned 10 world records in track and field events, has a bachelor's degree in education for the deaf and a master's degree in education for deaf and blind children. Marla also co-wrote and released her autobiography in 2001, *No Finish Line: My Life As I See It.*

Marla, you have my undying respect as a gifted athlete who showed the world that being handicapped doesn't have to keep anyone from being a star.

My list of other Ganesha-heroes includes Helen Keller, FDR, Stephen Hawking and Christopher Reeve. Two other notables are ABC reporter Bob Woodruff and Hollywood's heartthrob, George Clooney. Woodruff and Clooney are the only ones on this list with serious head injuries. They are also public figures who are bringing attention to TBI problems. Two living examples whose books and movies motivate millions to make a full recovery.

Bob Woodruff
In 2006, while working as a reporter in Iraq, Bob Woodruff was nearly killed when a roadside bomb struck his vehicle. He was placed in a medically-induced coma for 36 days so his brain could rest and recover. Bob underwent nine surgeries, one of which included the removal of part of his skull to relieve the intense pressure on his brain.

After surgery, it took a cognitive rehabilitation program for him to regain the mental skills he had lost. Woodruff still suffers from aphasia (the inability to find words, often caused by brain damage). He still has difficulty finding words, is blind in the upper quarter of both eyes and has lost a lot of his hearing.

In 2007, Bob and his wife Lee published a book called *In an Instant: A Family's Journey of Love and Healing.*

Today, Bob has recovered enough to resume his journalistic career. He and his wife have started a non-profit foundation, www.remind.org, to help veterans returning from war zones with brain injuries.

Bob is helping others with the same problem and has inspired me to write this book. After all, when you've been through a similar injury and ongoing recovery, you want to share the tools that worked for you.

George Clooney
After getting a serious brain injury during the filming of a fight scene, Clooney got such excruciating headaches that he considered committing suicide to escape the intense pain.

"It was the most unbearable pain I've ever been through," Clooney said, according to MSNBC.com. "Literally, where you'd go, 'Well, you'll have to kill yourself at some point because you can't live like this.'"

Like most TBI victims, Clooney has also suffered from embarrassing short-term memory loss. Since his TBI, he has been encouraging his memory to return by doing repetitive counting exercises.

"I have to work the memory muscle by counting everything, like how many times I pedal when I am on a bike," said Clooney. He stuck Post-It notes everywhere to remind him what's going on and described those 12 months as the worst year he has ever had.

To avoid drug addiction, Clooney didn't take conventional pain relievers. Instead, he opted for therapy that teaches him to ignore the pain. In spite of having some pain left, George has continued to soldier on bravely.

Even though his condition had worsened, Clooney attended the premiere of *Ocean's Twelve*. He promised his fans he would make a full recovery, saying, "I'll whip it. It's not permanent. It's a bruised brain. It's OK, it's going to be fine."

George was right—time makes all the difference. In 2013, he was the producer of *Argo,* which won the Academy Award for Best Picture.

Okay, pal, those are my current role models. Head injuries or not, they have two things in common—they've all overcome huge obstacles to achieve excellence, and none of them has let their disabilities get in their way.

Ganesha-heroes are being born every day—there are millions of stories out there. I'll close with this one which I found on CNN's online blog.

Hanna, Jason. *CNN News Blog,* May 1, 2012
Survivor of 2 Plane Crashes Still Intends to Play College Ball

Things were looking bright for 16-year-old Austin Hatch as last summer began. The Indiana boy who had survived a plane crash that killed his mother and two siblings eight years earlier had just verbally committed to playing basketball for the University of Michigan in 2013.

Then the 6-foot, 6-inch high school basketball star boarded another small plane bound for the family's summer home in Michigan. That plane crashed as it approached a Michigan airport on June 24, 2011, this time killing his father and stepmother.

Austin survived again, but now with brain bruising and other injuries, and without any immediate family members. He was in a medically induced coma for weeks and underwent months of physical therapy.

This week, he told the Detroit Free Press that he'll still be on Michigan's team when the 2013-2014 season begins.

"I'm still going on a full basketball scholarship," Austin told the Free Press for a story published Tuesday. "I'll still be on the team and all of that and go to practice and everything. But I just don't know if I'll be quite as good as I was before. But I still have over a year until then, so a lot can happen."

Austin, of Canterbury High School in Fort Wayne, Indiana, sat out all of his junior season. Released from a rehabilitation hospital last fall, he speaks slower than he used to and hasn't yet been cleared to play basketball. But he says his brain is almost as sharp as it was, and says he has the backing of Michigan coach John Beilein, who can't comment publicly about Austin until he signs a letter of intent this fall, the Free Press reported.

"[Beilein] is one of the best guys that I know. He's unbelievable," Austin told the Free Press. "He says you're not

going to be as good at basketball—not yet. It takes time. He understands my road to recovery is not going to be an easy one."

Inspiring examples like the ones above help you set new goals that are as exciting as your old goals—goals that make you proud every time you score. They can also help you find new ways to use your natural talents. Become your own Ganesha-hero role model. Reaching new goals will not only lighten up your dark days, they'll help your dreams come true.

Chapter 16
New Goals

Everybody from Wall Streeters to coaches, teachers to soldiers and parents to bosses know that big challenges are far more motivating than small ones. They know that starting bigger means ending bigger, and that people who set high bars are glad they did.

The analogies are endless. Winning the game means going for a rout. Getting B's means studying for A's. Winning an amateur title means training like a pro, and writing a best-seller means going for a good book.

Back in 1993 I was very excited about returning to a creative job in advertising. I had an interview for the Creative Director job of McCann-Erickson's Asia-Pacific division. It was all set, but the next day, that damn truck made it impossible.

Two years later, I needed a new goal to stay sane, a way to do what I've always been good at. A way to feel prideful again. But mainly I needed a goal I could accomplish despite of my new limitations.

I figured if Lance Armstrong, Bob Woodruff and George Clooney could do it, I could too. I figured if Austin Hatch could return to college basketball after two plane crashes and a serious

TBI, and if millions of unknown survivors could do it every day, so could I.

Since so little is known about recovering or living with a TBI and so few survivors are as lucky as I am, I decided to write this book about my first-hand experiences. I felt that other survivors shouldn't have to learn the hard way and voilà, my new goal was born.

Naturally, you can't score as many goals as you used to, but a good way to stay as goal-oriented as you ever were is by having fewer and more focused ones. You no longer have time or energy to do everything well, but don't worry about it, neither does anyone else.

These days you just have to be choosier. You no longer have the drive to waste on maybes. It's time for absolutes, definites and for sures. You'll need them for the work you have to do and the fun you want to have.

Once you've accepted this new reality, you're in luck, because there's a great way to make your new goals are as exciting as your old goals ever were. It involves setting the bar as high as you can.

Setting a high bar not only means your new goals will be satisfying, but soaring over that bar for the first time is a great feeling. The best thing about reaching it once is that you can reach it again and again and again. One day you won't even notice that you're taking the new height for granted. And you'll have learned an important lesson.

If I can do it once, I can do it again.

New goals are very important—you just need some new expectations to go with them.

I know a highly respected doctor of radiology, Dr. Wade Justice, whose recent brain injury has caused him to stop practicing medicine. His insurance company was so worried that he no longer processes information quickly enough, they refused to re-issue his malpractice policy.

Even though his TBI turned his life upside-down, he didn't waste time moping around or feeling sorry for himself. No, he changed his goals from being a more successful doctor to becoming a highly respected teacher. I figured if Dr. Justice could find new goals that were as exciting as his old goals, goddamn it, I could too.

These days, he's happily using his knowledge-base as professor of radiology at the Pacific Northwest University of Health Sciences. He's proudly teaching doctors several subjects that took him 30 years to learn. As he says, "My new goals have turned out to be every bit as exciting as my old ones."

I'm sure your old goals were very satisfying when you could deliver on them. Unfortunately, your brain is sending slower and sleepier signals, signals that have to be woken up with demanding new goals. These new goals will then be satisfying and effective at the same time.

You start by accepting that medical and psychological averages are exactly that—*averages*. Statistics simply give busy doctors a fast way to deal with anxious patients. But again, industry stats are just that—*stats*. And statistics are convenient and directional at best.

But you're no statistic. If you're finding that even several years after your injury, you're still stuck with your tired old goals—relax. It takes several years to realize those dusty old challenges have become worthless antiques. Why even bother dusting them off when we can get some shiny new ones?

Reaching most goals don't give you the great feeling that comes with vaulting over a high bar. You don't get the satisfaction of looking up and seeing a pole that's still rattling on its brackets or hearing the applause of an enthusiastic audience.

The dictionary defines a goal as the "result or achievement toward which effort is directed." But that definition isn't personal enough, is it? No, you need goals that are about *you* and you alone, goals that are directed at shortening your recovery time.

The best way to do this is to make goals out of overcoming your limitations. That way the very symptoms that hold you back become challenges instead of obstacles. It's a double.

The dictionary also defines goal as "an endeavor that involves establishing short-or long-term objectives, usually incorporating deadlines and quantifiable measures."

Deadlines and quantifiable measures are both very important. Quantifiable measures are just a fancy way of saying testable, and there's nothing like a test score to give you solid proof that your goal has been achieved. Since your current life is all about mini-goals, you need that proof more than ever.

Like the proof that's right on your wrist, hanging in your bathroom or right underfoot. Think about it—the stopwatch never lies, the mirror can't lie and the scale always tells the absolute truth.

But seriously, these really are good tests because they all give you tangible proof of success. Proof you just can't fake. Proof like less time on the stopwatch, looking trimmer in the mirror or the little arrow that says you dropped a couple pounds.

There are scads of memory tests in newspapers and magazines and plenty of books on the subject, but the best ones always come from real life.

Every time you don't need a reminder or an aid of any kind, give yourself a score.

Give yourself a "C" for being on time, a "B" for remembering your partner or spouse's birthday and an "A" for remembering your anniversary.

Pretty soon you'll be graduating *summa cum laude*.

All tests should also have deadlines. Not the kind that are imposed by bosses, clients or organizations, but self-imposed deadlines like telling yourself you have to get something done by the weekend, by the close of business or before you go on vacation. The best deadlines are the deadlines you make for yourself.

Deadlines are very motivating because as soon as you set them, your goals have an urgency that didn't exist before. Deadlines make your mini-victories real because there's now a target date with a tangible finality.

Getting raises, earning promotions and setting records may be about success, but passing your own tests is all about *freedom*. The freedom of not needing aids, crutches or help of any kind. The freedom of independence. The freedom of having challenging new goals. The freedom of doing it your way.

Your new goals will cost you more than your old goals ever did. So what? Going for the gold always takes you further.

But hey, new goals are just dreams without the right motivation. The next chapter has tips about using anger, scheduling your day, rewarding yourself and, most important of all, tips about taking risks. If you can boost your motivation, you can get what you want.

Chapter 17
New Motivation

So pal, since the right motivation is extremely personal, I figured I'd start with a few tips of what's worked for me with the hopes that it might work for you, too. The right motivation will help your goals become reality.

Mondays

I've had to accept that my new goals would be fantasies forever unless I took a new look at what charges me up. So I started with my favorite day of the week—Monday!

I've always thought Monday was the most motivating day of the week. A day that signals five more days of hope and promise. A day to get excited about the week ahead. A day to swear a blood oath to the god of completion.

Hey, the only thing that's more motivating than making a weekly plan on Monday is sticking to it until Sunday.

Being Early

Getting up early and showing up early has to be next. My father always told me to get to work before anyone else. When I asked him what I would do in there that early, he always said, "You'll think of something."

Even though I hate admitting he was right, I always had my best ideas in that total vacuum. By the time everybody else staggered into the office, the phones started ringing and the voices started shrilling, I was ready.

Staying Busy

I can remember when staying busy not only passed the time, but the adrenaline rush I got from it created momentum. I used to complete about a dozen different jobs before lunch. And that momentum snowballed, creating more momentum.

In advertising, doing creative work and ducking bullets at the same time meant I had to get organized. I used to have an illegible daily schedule and a desktop full of crumpled scrawling. Most of the time I couldn't even understand them, and when I did I would forget to put them in my calendar anyway.

It became an office joke.

I finally graduated to making organized lists in pocket notebooks and leaving all kinds of weird reminders. I still remember how checking those things off my list gave me a sense of accomplishment. In fact, I'm still doing it today.

Luckily, I liked my job enough to see my lists as challenges rather than havta's and gotta's.

These days it's much easier to get organized with smart phones, day books, online planners and even Post-Its. Whatever system you use, crossing things off your list is especially motivating when you have a TBI, because it makes you want to check off what's next.

Taking Risks

Anyone with a life or death job will tell you that they're highly motivated by risk. Soldiers, firemen, sky divers, bullfighters, lifeguards and bodyguards all know that nothing spurs them on like the fear of death. They actually get hooked on it.

But I'm not a bullfighter, so what's risk got to do with a TBI recovery? Plenty. The anxiety that comes with risk creates uncertainties about the future, uncertainties that force me to ad-lib through life instead of relying on stale mental scripts. Taking risks actually gives my brain thousands of harmless mini-traumas. It makes me ask questions like, *Will I get there in time? Will I make it? Will I be okay? Can I do this tomorrow?*

Answering these questions has not only given me reassurance, it has sped up my recovery time.

Risk creates intense neural activity that makes my brain rewire, and that rewiring creates new neural pathways. Risk has given me countless automatic responses that calls for immediate action. Taking risks has sped up my brain's recovery process by increasing its capability.

But we don't need to use intense risk to make the point. Commonplace risks like learning to ride a bike again, walking down stairs without using the railing, taking your first solo drive or eating in public for the first time work just as well.

Risk has also gotten me out of the doldrums. It's given me some adrenaline rushes. It's woken me up. It's taken me from could-be's to have-to-be's.

You should learn to love risk too. It's not only a lot faster than repetition, it will stop your mind from floating around in yesterday and land it in the now.

Attacking!

After the crash, it didn't take long for retreat to become a bad habit. Retreat was an automatic, chicken-shit response to difficulties. But I've always believed that attacking works better than retreating every time and being aggressive by nature, I feel good about making attacks my first response. Simply put, my TBI symptoms became an enemy I had to defeat.

Attacking should become your first response, too. During the last 22 years, I've attacked my embarrassment, my limitations and the things that scare me by charging straight into the lion's den of my fears.

Attacking has worked big time! The sooner I began to choose fight over flight, the sooner I forgot about retreating. I still remember running around a really scary parcourse, a fitness trail of a measured mile that was dusted over with loose dirt and gravel on steep, twisty hills. At first, I saw myself as a victim of a killer course that would trip and tear me up if I wasn't careful.

But since a strong offense really is the best defense, I soon realized I would never get around that grinder any faster if I didn't embrace risk. So I began to time every run and try to do it faster every day. I had to see speeding up and down those rocky hills as a risk worth taking. And as soon as I loved the risk, I stopped being scared. I also stopped tripping, got less bloody and my times get faster and faster.

I credit that parcourse with a huge part of my physical recovery and it will always be the place where I got better because taking risks worked for me.

My behavioral therapist always urged me to try a new thing every day. Even trying old skills again, like biking, would speed up my relearning process.

She was right.

Since I could no longer handle a real racer with skinny tires and shoe clips, I got a big heavy cruiser that reminded me of my first red Schwinn. It was heavy as hell with wide, red fenders over balloon tires and white-walls, but at least it was a bike.

What followed was months of clockwise and counter-clockwise circles around my driveway. Boring as hell, but since it was a blacktop driveway and my balance was gone, the risk of falling off and hitting my head again was very real.

So what's so motivating about that?

While I was making those boring circles around the driveway, I found myself yearning to ride on the open road and wishing for a cooler bike, hot shoes and aerodynamic clothes. I was even yearning for the day I wouldn't even think about using the bike for transportation. Those yearnings were so motivating, I decided to attack riding this new bike like I attacked the parcourse.

Good thing, because that bike-attack helped me go from scary rides to mini-victories, from scary mini-victories to routine rides, and from routine rides to fun. Now when I throw a leg over that bike's saddle, it feels like I'm going on an adventure with an old friend.

So, pal, the lesson is this: if you can turn retreat into a bad habit and attack into a reflexive response, you'll notice the difference on day one.

Ongoing Responsibilities

It may sound obvious, but few things are as motivating as an ongoing responsibility. This is especially true of a highly visible one. Coaching a high school team, becoming a Scout Master or joining the Big Brother program are good examples. But, since I prefer to stick to myself, I created an ongoing website called www.philslott.com.

I originally posted it to be discovered by a good literary agent, but even though that has finally happened, I still have a stage to perform on.

Since I can't turn my advertising mind off, it's fun to see if I've still got it, so I keep writing and posting new campaigns for whatever comes into my head. Needless to say it's been a very motivating exercise.

Here's one for the nearby prep school where we would walk around the track:

The world's best climate for growth.

Since a drunk driver nearly killed me, I took a crack at this one for Mothers Against Drunk Driving (MADD):

We try not to be famous last words.

My friend Sylvia asked me to name her spa-design business:

S.P.A.
Sylvia **P**lanning **A**nd Design

This one was for my wife's ocean swim team, the Lane 1 Swim Team:

There are no lanes in the ocean.

This one was done in '09 for a newly minted homeopathic physician:

We're never too busy to care.

And, hell, this damn thing just popped into my head:

We try not to come between you.
Trojan Contraceptives

Rewards

Since everything in life is more work than it used to be, rewarding myself is a great perk. Self-rewards are more than just satisfying—they motivate me to work harder and give me the incentive to win my next reward.

Rewarding myself doesn't have to be like winning the grand prize on a quiz show—it can be as simple as hugging myself, reaching around to pat myself on the back, or just yelling, "GOOD JOB!" out loud.

Social Pressure

When you think about it, social pressure is one of man's biggest motivators. Social pressure will never be as motivating as survival. But when it comes to a TBI recovery, it's damn near as motivating as the need for food and shelter. Really!

Being concerned about how we look in front of others is a useful tool. Social pressure not only demands that we look good and do our best, it keeps us from looking bad and doing our worst. I have to admit that social pressure drives me all day and keeps me on top of my game.

My best two examples of social pressure in action happened a number of years after the crash. One was in a sword-training class and the other was a presentation to the marketing department at the preparatory high school near our home.

Before the crash, I spent years training in a traditional form of Japanese combat technique called Yagy Shinkage-ry , one of the oldest schools of swordsmanship in Japan. Yagy focuses on the use of weapons like the sword, the spear and the halbert. The idea is to win by making your opponent unable to fight without killing him.

Even before my injuries, the Yagy training sessions were physically and mentally intense. After the crash, it took a long time before I was even willing to show up.

When I finally did, I made up my mind to be very aggressive in my first sword-training session. Amazingly, I was able to keep pressing the attack all the way through some furious *katas*, special

Yagy exercises and techniques. All my opponents were surprised, and they gave me a barefoot ovation when we finished.

Sword training put me to the test physically and mentally, but the job for Hawaii Preparatory Academy put my old presentation and marketing skills to the creative test. I did the consulting job for free because I was only interested in re-proving myself as a sound advertising mind and a good presenter. After attending several strategy meetings with their staff, I worked up about 20 different signature lines for the school.

The idea was for them to think of themselves as a brand, one that used a single identity-phrase on everything from their stationery to a sign on the front gate.

My recommendation was *The World's Best Climate for Growth*, which I thought was right on for a leading prep school in Hawaii. The marketing group liked it so much that they gave me an enthusiastic round of applause.

Both of these moments were highly motivating because they spurred me on to try for more atta-boys. Anytime you can get a cheer, pal, get it—because one cheer makes you want another.

Showing Off

Nobody likes a show off—especially me.

I've always thought of them as egocentric assholes I never wanted to be. But even though that's still true, I've come to believe that a little showing off can be quite motivating from time to time.

An occasional display of excellence is more than proof to others—it's proof to yourself. This solid proof can boost your self-confidence. Like social pressure, showing off will make you want to do your best. Like risk, it forces you to relearn. And, like rewards, it's fun.

Showing off can do more harm than good if you're not modest about it. Bragging and blowing your own horn take a lot of work, using up resources you can't afford to spare, so that should be out! After all, you know when you've done it well and so will they.

Flirting

Flirting is a great motivator because it's amplified by strong emotions. Like showing off, it pushes me to look my best. It involves relearning, rewards and fun.

Showing off does an acceptable job of displaying my skills and talents, but flirting actually uses my appearance, wardrobe, personality and charms (such as they are).

Flirting means trading compliments instead of information, hugs instead of anecdotes and long looks instead of short stories. I'm strutting my stuff instead of strutting my skills. And hey, I may not hear the applause, but I can feel it.

When you think about it, flirting is showing off *plus.* I think of it as a personal and romantic victory at the same time. It not only affirms, confirms and builds my confidence, it's proof I've still got the same old stuff. And what could be more motivating than that!

Of course, flirting has the same warning labels as showing off and only a fool would ignore them.

Social Networking

Flirting is highly motivating, but maybe you're not up for singles' bars, ski resorts, shopping malls or driving to weekends at the beach.

Lucky us, because today's technology has given us social networking. Social networking is a great way to flirt right from home.

These days the web can not only create daily companionship, it starts and maintains thousands of real relationships. Some of these end in job offers, many become life-long friendships and even a few of them of them end in marriage. Visiting sites like

Twitter and eHarmony are faster, easier and cheaper ways to find a lasting relationship than a singles cruise ever will be.

Books and Movies

I've always enjoyed reading books and watching movies for entertainment. But these days, they've gone from welcome escapes to motivating recovery tools.

It's all due to the creative geniuses who bring their heroes to life, from Tom Wolfe's crash-and-burn freight loaders to Robert Crais' Cole-Pike partnership. Look at screenwriters like Ann Biderman, actors like Rupert Everett and TV directors like Michael Mann—these brilliant people not only keep me entertained, they bring me heroes that teach by example, guys who go for it when the going gets tough.

Books and movies also bring cowards to life, characters who retreat instead of attack. Characters who crumble in the face of obstacles are valuable since they show me what not to be.

There are lots of good reasons to go to more movies, read more books and watch more well-written TV series. But the most important reason is that they help me see myself in tense situations without the anxiety that goes with them.

Vanity

Fess up, guys. We care as much about our appearance as the women in our lives. We're not only as snowed by the same expensive TV commercials and slick magazine ads, we buy just as many fashion, diet and fitness guides as they do. And we've been wearing expensive colognes and bikini underwear for years.

Luckily, these fantasies have been man-ized by the most brilliant advertising industry in the world. Highly paid, super-talented creative people make sure that vanity for men is a completely natural development. What used to be the sole province of women has just become another male habit—unisex is no longer a fad or a trend, it's an assumption.

What does all this interest in grooming, wardrobe and fragrance have to do with motivation? It's simple. TBIs often come with symptoms like sloppiness, confusion, angry outbursts, short-term memory loss, fuzzy thinking and disorientation. These symptoms make us look incompetent and out of control. They make us say goodbye to the smooth-talking heartthrob who's never embarrassed because he's always in control. Now we have to say hello to the red-faced dufus who's always embarrassed because he's never in control.

As a result, we red-faced dufuses need a strong dose of the right motivation every day. Vanity helps do the job. And when we look better, we do better.

Vanity is not just for hot dates, either—it helps us win in the game of life. Vanity helps us impress our wives, compete with our co-workers and be confident outside when we feel insecure inside. Vanity not only helps us feel important again, it makes sure we get taken seriously and leads to as much social acceptance as we deserve. It even urges us to keep fit.

So the next time you don't like what you see in the gym mirror, don't worry, let vanity come to the rescue.

Dumping Aids
Nothing was as motivating as watching my tired, old physical aids sliding down the chute at the Waimea town dump. I can still remember laughing during those mock-funeral ceremonies— saying goodbye to those worn-out canes, crutches, braces and walkers and saying hello to freedom!

The same has been true of dumping my brain injury aids. Over the years, I've had some amusing ceremonies for them, too. I'd stand over my own wastepaper can, holding a mock ceremony for wrinkled stickies, wordy prescription warnings, scrawled lists and unneeded reminders.

Saying goodbye to unneeded aids is more than a great feeling—it's highly motivating. If you make it your number one goal, you'll enjoy funerals for the first time in your life. Ashes to ashes...

Dressing for the Part

We all have special outfits for church, weddings, funerals and the office. These outfits do all kinds of different jobs, from getting us into the right mood to showing respect, from helping us feel casual to making us look business-like, from making us feel athletic to making us look academic.

Most people see the right outfit as clothes that are appropriate for the occasion. They'd never go to a funeral in shorts, an important meeting in resort wear or look sloppy at a friend's wedding.

But the most important reason of all? The right clothes are *very* motivating.

What about sports? Tennis and golf clubs have all kinds of strict dress requirements, but gyms don't have any dress codes at all. Since gyms don't have dress codes it means you often see people in their worst clothes, sometimes the same ones they worked out in the day before.

This is especially true of guys. Many show up in the over-the-calf socks they wore to work, not to mention dirty shorts and wrinkled T-shirts. It looks like their outfits are still sweaty from the last time.

Women are neater, but their decisions are usually based on what they think looks slimming or what's in fashion that year. Luckily, timeless black outfits are both fashionable and slimming, even if they don't have anything to do with a hard workout.

Wearing the right stuff in the gym goes beyond vanity or social pressure. Suiting up motivates me by making me feel determined, like I sure as hell better live up to my outfit. And showing others I'm serious makes me feel serious.

Mild Stimulants

In spite of the above motivational tips, when it comes to an intense work out I need all the help I can get. And as much as I love the gym, I need drugs.

Drugs to wake me up from my daily nap. Drugs to help me get to the gym. Drugs to motivate me while I'm working out.

In the early years after my crash, doctors were sure very strong stimulants would do the job. They would help extend my day and give me the energy to get out and about.

Good idea, I thought. *It's as simple as taking a pill!*

I tried that approach but it only took one workout for me to realize that too much stimulation from very strong drugs was a bad idea. Strong drugs over-activated my damaged brain and caused anger and confusion. This was followed by a terrible emotional crash and intense fatigue.

Not good.

Strong stimulants were too much work for my system, but the benefits from mild stimulants have been terrific. They helped me focus and kept my mind on the job without the unpleasant side effects.

Remember how my doctor initially prescribed two small doses of Ritalin a day? And that it took years of trial and error to realize that an A.M. and P.M. dose was just too much speed for a single day? Since I don't need any incentive in the morning, I switched to P.M. doses only. Even though the positive effects of Ritalin vary from day to day, it works for me.

A 5 mg dose not only improves my overall coordination, it gives me a positive attitude and improves my drive. The stuff works like a five-hour booster shot and when I add a commercial energy-booster like Shot-Blok, it's almost like a recreational drug. And then you've got coffee, energy bars and protein powder which also give you some extra fuel for the rest of the day. How cool is that?

If the old you loved the gym, mild stimulants are not only very motivating, they'll help the new you love it all over again.

Get a Blog or Website

Not everybody sees themselves as a writer or can afford their own website, but these days it's easy to set up a simple website or blog for free on Wordpress, Blogger or Tumblr. As long as you have a computer, you can have a Facebook page or just keep close friends posted with your current opinions or just telling them what's new by sending out a regular email once a week.

Whether it's personal or professional, maintaining your own site is very motivating, because of the exposure and social pressure involved. The daily maintenance will keep you busy. And most importantly, it gives you a place to show off.

The Right Music

History tells us that music has been motivating people for centuries. From national anthems to waltzes. From military marches to cha-cha-chas. From church choirs to wild raves. From displaying loyalty, faith and patriotism to boosting morale. Music has been motivating people for millions of years in thousands of different ways.

These days, strong music is still motivating soldiers with marching bands, stirring football crowds with aggressive chants, motivating purchases with unforgettable jingles and making worshippers feel that they've chosen the right religion.

Marches, chants and jingles all get the job done, but I'm not in the Army anymore, this isn't half-time and I'm happy with the products I've already got. What motivates me today is the music I love.

Music that gets me beyond the pettiness of the day so I can get excited about life and the ideas that make it worthwhile. Music that connects me to some larger truths, that lets me touch my emotions in a safe way.

Melodies that makes me close my eyes, rhythms that quicken my heartbeat and lyrics I'll never forget. Truthful music by bluesmen like BB King and Eric Clapton. Grassroots music by country gals like Emmy Lou Harris, Linda Ronstadt and Brandi Carlisle. Heart-stopping music by great singers like Toni Childs, Susan Tedeschi, Chris Isaacs, the Dixie Chicks and Faith Hill. Kick-ass music by John Fogarty, Creedence Clearwater, George Thorogood in the good old days and the brilliant songs by Bonnie Raitt today.

But the most motivating music of all is the passionate music by Beth Hart, Adele, any number of Latin singers or my favorite group, the Gypsy Kings.

Hearing the music I love is not only as motivating as hell, it's a fun way to be around artists who are dedicated to excellence.

Of course, sometimes hearing the best music is as simple as going to the movies. Think about it—a good score is as worthwhile as the movie it comes from. The best ones can become motivating soundtracks for your life.

If music can motivate millions of true believers, vast armies, drunk fans, screaming teenagers and eager consumers, it stands to reason that the right music can motivate you to do the hard work that's in front of you every day.

Hard work? Hold on, I thought music was supposed to be fun! *Eureka,* that's the whole point! The truth is that most successful recoveries *are* fun.

It doesn't matter what kind of music motivates you. Maybe it's listening to today's cool rock or yesterday's beautiful arias. All that matters is that it gets you going.

It doesn't matter if you're a waiter with a tray full of fragile dishes, a landscaper with dirty hands or a venture capitalist with millions on the line. All the motivational techniques in this chapter can be very useful if you learn or relearn how to use them.

Music aside? I don't think so. You might be able to can recover without it, but I can't.

Maybe you're more motivated by taking risks than getting rewards. Maybe you're less motivated by social pressure than head-on attacks. Maybe you're motivated by getting mad. Or maybe you're just as motivated by vanity as by showing off. No problem. Motivation varies from person to person, but we're all motivated when we hear the right words.

Chapter 18
The Right Words

If you talk to yourself as much as I do, using the right words is very important.

Let's get the wrong words out of the way forever: *Can't, scared, crazy, lazy, tired, angry, anxious, demented* and the two S-words, *sorry* and *suicide*.

Gone!

Next let's lose the words *handicapped, depressed, quit* and *victim* unless they're followed by the words *not, never* or *hate*.

Good!

Now we can talk to ourselves like this:

I AM <u>*NOT*</u> HANDICAPPED!

Trust me, when it comes to recovering, negative language can be highly motivating. It's far more motivating to deny being handicapped than it is to accept it.

Denial leads to action, acceptance leads to inertia. Denial cries out for change, acceptance settles for the status quo. Denial puts you on offense, acceptance keeps you on defense. Denial is bullish, acceptance is bearish. Denial takes you where you want to go, acceptance leaves you where you are.

An example:

I'LL NEVER QUIT UNTIL THE JOB IS DONE.

Very few statements make you feel as positive as the ones that deny the negative, so let's add a few more to make the point.

I NEVER GET DEPRESSED.

Fighting depression is as simple as denying any glass is ½ empty.

I NEVER LOOK BACK.

Too many victims are stuck in the past. They keep acting like patients long after their injuries are healed. Looking back keeps reminding them of their victim days so they never really recover.

No matter how much better you get, you should always look forward to getting *more* better.

I NEVER WASTE TIME.

It's very motivating to realize that if you keep sitting around, you might never get up. Conventional wisdom says accident victims should wait until they feel better before they get active.

Bullshit! If you want to improve, you should get up and do it RIGHT NOW. I do it by making sure I do U-turns if I'm on the wrong route.

There's really no such thing as a red-letter day after a traumatic crash. But one thing that always gets me going is knowing that everything stinks and I'm better off doing anything than I am doing nothing.

Denial and negative language work for me, but the right positive statements work, too.

I GET BETTER EVERY DAY.

Doing a task better this week than seven days ago is a progress day. I find progress days are very motivating because they demand more progress days.

I'VE GOT A NEW CAREER.

Living with a brain injury is a full-time job and I already had a full-time job—writing. It was time for me to think of recovery as a new career, and it was time for my two jobs to motivate each other. It was time to feel proud about multi-tasking.

So think of it this way, pal—you don't have a handicap, you have a new career. A whole array of interesting new tasks to keep you busy. There's nothing like staying busy to keep depression away.

MEMORY DRILLS ARE FUN.

Anytime I could turn overcoming an obstacle into a game, I did it by playing the memory game. It works like this: Try to recall obscure parts of your early life—like making forts in kindergarten, archery at summer camp, summer jobs or the good meals you had on dates. Have fun remembering Army lectures, co-workers' names, your friends' birthdays, etc.

Here's a tip that helps me remember these moments. I take a break by *not* thinking about my overall problem. This causes my mind to relax and *Eureka!* My old memories come back stronger than ever.

Recalling the distant past is fun, and if you force yourself to recall the more recent days, weeks and months, it will be harder but even more useful. The Memory Game not only builds memory-power, there's a big AHA! when the details come back.

I'M FLEXIBLE.

Flexibility bends the success curve in the right direction. If something isn't working, it pays to change it quickly. I always found that changing my program can be very motivating. A changed program is an updated program, an updated program leads to progress and making progress always has made me feel good. Flexibility works as long as we both remember not to change too much too fast.

I'M TOUGH-MINDED.

The best way to get tough-minded was by believing that I was. I convinced myself that compromising was losing, that my fears were only obstacles and that my imperfections were just challenges.

It worked! It was only a matter of time until they were all overcome.

I think you'll find aggressiveness is the most effective state of mind. It really pays to make a straw man you can knock down (and straw men are very flammable).

I HAVE BIG GOALS.

Most behavioral therapists will tell you that TBI victims need more modest goals, but I never bought it. Seems to me that the bigger the goal, the bigger the victory. And I never forget that I'm no victim—I'm a survivor. Goddammit, we're both survivors!

I LOVE TAKING RISKS.

Owning a home truth like *no risk, no reward* has never been more important than it is right now. There's just no such thing as a solid recovery without taking a lot of chances. I've just had to accept risk as a fact of daily life.

Anyone who loves dangerous sports will tell you that taking risks is exponential. The more risks you take, the more you need them, and this leads to more risk taking. Eventually you get hooked on risk.

But most rehab centers are so worried about lawsuits from new injuries that they play it safe, and that's too bad, because it means that many of our future heroes are lost forever.

I LOVE ADVENTURE.

Adventures are thrilling, but they wouldn't be called adventures if they weren't more challenging than everyday life. The old me loved them. But these days, the risk and uncertainty that comes with an adventure seems a lot more stressful. When I think of them as growth opportunities, they not only become exciting all over again, they're uplifting.

Exciting, because they actually increase my capabilities. I remember the first plane ride I took by myself after the crash. Even though the plane was packed, it felt like a solo flight.

A half-hour flight from Honolulu to Kona may not sound like much, but dealing with the details of the trip by myself did a lot for me. Coping with simple things like busy airports, checking in, urgent warnings, gate changes and more urgent warnings sound like a pain in the ass, and they would have been if they weren't so useful.

That same trip was uplifting because I thought of it as an adventure instead of work, as a kind of a game instead of a scary ordeal. As a result, I stopped dreading travel and began to see the experience as a test I was proud to pass.

Proud of dealing with the stress. Proud of being spontaneous. Proud of being confident. So proud to be independent that it made me want to do it again and again.

To say it was a fun trip would be going too far, but seeing it as an adventure turned an anxious event into the same boring routine I always thought it was.

Transforming your scary challenges into adventures will make them far less scary too, and I hope you find an adventure around every corner.

Can-do words like *fun, flexible, tough, adventure, risk* and *reward* feel much better than can't-do words. But words are only words. It's time to stop talking and start doing. It's time for us to follow my father's advice:

"Just put one foot in front of the other."

Over the years I've taken his words so seriously they've become a full-time attitude. An aggressive, action-oriented attitude that's been key to my recovery.

My dad's advice got me out of that damned wheelchair, helped me throw away those embarrassing canes, walkers and crutches and it gave me a *go-for-it* attitude. An attitude that calls for shouting YES! followed by an enthusiastic fist pump!

Hey, pal, I'm sure if he were still alive today he'd want us both to believe these next five words most of all:

I AM NOT A VICTIM.

Chapter 19
The Right Stuff

Thousands of earnest books, documentaries and organizations have been created to motivate people. Unfortunately, they don't talk about how the right *stuff*, as in things, can help, too. Too bad. Nothing has ever motivated me as much as hearing the right words, but owning the right stuff runs a close second.

I had to learn by doing, but having the right stuff helped a lot—it actually insisted that I do my best. In fact, the right stuff has always demanded that I respect it by using it the right way. Sometimes I can even hear it calling.

The Catholic Church has always known this. Centuries of priests have been teaching the faithful that human and spiritual realities are actually embodied in three-dimensional symbols. Symbols you can touch, like crucifixes, goblets and statues. Symbols you can taste, like wine and wafers. Symbols you can wear, like robes, rings and sashes. Not to mention incense you can smell, music you can hear, inspiring stained glass windows and priceless ceilings you can look at.

Even symbolic gestures are connected to the right stuff. Gestures like making the sign of the cross, being blessed with holy water, kneeling, bowing or lying prostrate.

Of course every ideology believes that basic truths are more important than the right stuff or making the right gestures. But it seems to me, they not only depend on each other, they were born at the same time.

Religion isn't the only example. Back when I had hot cars, they were always inviting me to go for a drive. High-performance bikes were always daring me to ride them. And cool trainers were always challenging me to go for a run. They were out there in the garage yelling, "Drive me!" "Ride me!" and "Run with me!" Since brain injuries steal so much energy, these challenges are still what I need to hear.

So what exactly is the right stuff for tough times? That took a while to learn. When it comes to athletics, I believe the right stuff is the equipment that's made for stiff competition. Stuff like racing-quality, competition-ready, varsity-sanctioned or official pro gear. Gear like an aerodynamic bike helmet, professional boxing gloves and serious brands like Nike, Everlast and Champion.

But before I could hear this stuff calling for me to work out, I had to have it first. I wanted to get it before I needed it, so it would have enough time to seduce me. And, like any other spouse, once I had its number it insisted on full respect. It insisted that I would never let it down. It insisted that I was never lazy. And, it insisted that I deserved it by proving it with my best performance.

Forward-canted trainers insist that you run faster. Low-slung sports cars urge you to make sharper turn. And the right brands make you proud to suit up.

Everybody has their own idea about what makes the right stuff the right stuff right. Here's mine:

The Right Board
The only other spouse that's as captivating as Mary is my authentic, three-string long board. I love that thing so much, I used to make special trips to the garage just to admire it. It had such a demanding

personality, I swear I could almost hear it yelling, "Hey, Phil, it's honkin' big out there—let's get wet!"

Even though I haven't really surfed since 1993, that board is still waiting for me out in the garage. I've never been the jealous type, so if you ever want to check it out, let me know. But nobody rides it except me.

The Right Mitt

A few years after the crash, my friend Leo gave me a baseball glove so we could have a catch when I got better. But it wasn't just any old mitt. No way. Leo went out and found a Reach Pro Model with a built-in pocket.

Catch, hell—that glove insisted we make dazzling catches, that we thrill the crowd with perfect plays and that we shout 'em out like the ol' redhead Red Barber used to do.

The Right Watch

I used to have a diving watch that was a lot more than amphibious. I wore that yellow G-Shock surfing, running, gymming and everywhere else.

It was also a stopwatch and before I knew it, I was setting measured running and swimming distances and timing them every day. This not only made my workouts more interesting, it turned them into challenges. Challenges like setting new goals and trying to beat them.

I recently told Mary that I thought of my yellow watch as a symbol of our more active lifestyle, and that I missed those days. She found me another one for my birthday and our active lifestyle came back with it. Talk about the right stuff!

The Right Bike

Biking is all about a romantic affair with the right bike. In fact, my old racer had such a sexy body, I miss it like it was a hot Italian mistress. But no matter how much I'm pining away for its shiny black paint job, shapely frame, slim tires and the cleavage between its curvaceous drop-bars, it was just too unstable to ride anymore. It was too fragile, tippy and low slung. I had to kiss it goodbye.

I'm more steady on my new upright beach bike with its big fat tires, but I have a love-hate relationship with this new American mistress. No matter how hard she tries, I can't help pining away for my old lover.

The Right Gym Clothes

You know the gym is good for you. You know it makes you feel younger. You're sure it makes you slimmer. You can't wait for your old clothes to fit again. But maybe you're just too lethargic to get there. Your problem could be as simple not having the right clothes for the job.

The right clothes for the gym? Like most people, you're probably wearing your almost yellow T-shirts, your tired-looking shorts and your most squashed overshoes. It's not exactly Club Med in there.

Of course, you wouldn't even think of wearing the wrong clothes to weddings, funerals or the office. But you don't think of gym clothes in the same way. No, you figure it's just the smelly old gym so you might as well wear your worst. You throw on any old freebie T- shirt, yesterday's socks and the same baggy shorts you wore last time.

What are the right clothes? This is no advertorial, but it seems to me that your gym outfit should say that you're really serious about today's workout. That you're dressed for the part, that you feel official, that you feel professional and that you feel as cool as your new pair of Nike Air Force One's.

Wearing the right clothes is no substitute for willpower or having the right attitude. But dressing for the part in any field spurs you to re-prove yourself, and the gym is no exception. When you think about it, having an official gym outfit goes beyond practicality or social pressure. It actually helps you feel brisk and business-like,

like a professional who knows what he's doing. And hey, if they think you're a personal trainer, so be it.

There's only one problem left, but it's a class-A problem. The right gym clothes are a challenge. Now that you've taken the trouble to put them on, you have to live up to them. There's no way you're going to let down a pair of Air Max LeBron James shoes—you have to work hard to deserve them. Lifting more weight, doing more reps and lifting until you reach failure on every set.

Whether you admit it or not, looking right is showing off. Showing off makes your heart beat faster and showing off is very motivating. And the right outfit says I'm here because I *want* to be here, not because I *have* to be here.

Here's another booster shot that worked for me. I used to carry my surfboard, snowboard or skateboard in the bed of my truck every day until I hit ground zero.

When I finally recovered enough to drive, I wanted to keep on boarding, but I needed inspiration.

One day, I was staring into my truck's empty bed when it came to me. I figured that even though I'm not the vanity-plate type, what the hell—it might just do the trick.

A vanity plate, are you crazy?

Believe it or not, a vanity plate is a lot more than a silly piece of tin for egotistical assholes. The right one can motivate you. The right one can challenge you. The right one can put just enough social pressure on you. The right one can be the right stuff. And the right one can become a mantra for the new you.

As you read in Mary's chapter, this one's mine: 3 BRDS.

The Right Chair
A high-performance wheelchair is another good example. Even though I've been lucky enough not to need one, it's well worth

mentioning. Anybody who needs a wheelchair should test-drive it before they spend money on the hospital kind.

A disabled athlete can drive their chair with one arm so the other arm can shoot a basketball, make forehands and backhands, even fire a rifle. It's not logy or awkward in any way—it performs like a Porsche. A red-hot wheelchair with faster pick-up, excellent brakes and great suspension to make sharper turns.

Experienced operators can not only get to a volleyball slam in time, they can use this flashy chair to defeat the very limitations that have been holding them back. Having the right stuff means they can say goodbye to their low performance forever.

What does the wrong stuff tell us about the right stuff?

You can always tell when you blew it by what your stuff doesn't do. The wrong stuff doesn't challenge you to a workout. It doesn't ask you to have a catch. It doesn't dare you to go surfing, skateboarding, snowboarding. It doesn't challenge you to make tight turns, invite you to go for a run or just take a ride. In fact, you never hear it calling, because it never is. It never invites you to a party or challenges you in any way. It never makes you feel proud to own it. It doesn't seduce you, make you fall in love or leave you breathless.

Does your stuff make you feel sluggish, dazed, distracted, vegged-out, foggy, logy, listless or draggy? Does your stuff leave you debilitated and turned off, instead of enervated and turned on? If so, then you've got the wrong stuff.

The right stuff helps you overcome your natural resistance to anything that scares you, sort of like wearing the right gown to a ball or the right suit to a big presentation. The wrong stuff just sits there.

Living up to the right stuff is never easy. As soon as you get it, it raises your expectations and demands your best performance. The bar is set much higher.

Of course, having the right stuff goes far beyond athletics. Dress clothes make me want to go on a date. Cool designer furniture makes me want to redecorate. And I can almost hear my copper cookware complaining that I don't make enough gourmet recipes (not to mention, "Polish me!").

Every injury comes with the built-in desire to get over it, a strong urge that may be satisfied by putting an Air Force One shoe over a prosthetic foot. But the right stuff doesn't have to cost you a cent. All you need is the right attitude, drive and willpower it takes to stay fit.

Chapter 20
The New Fitness

The right stuff has really helped me get back on stage, but I couldn't take a bow until my laziness exited stage-left and my energy re-entered on stage-right.

Everybody knows that workouts are good for you, but since I have extensive brain damage, an ongoing program is critical. Workouts not only send much-needed oxygen to my brain, they stimulate the natural tranquilizer we know as endorphins.

The problem is exercise usually means playing games. But waiting for fly balls in the outfield, being lectured at half-time or clock-watching from the bench wastes too much time. Sports like tennis are more active, but even they take hours. Boxing is great exercise, but it's out since it might result in a second, and more serious, brain injury.

Not okay. The new me needed a new idea of fitness.

Why should I waste hours waiting to go into action when I could spend a half hour in constant action? Most experts agree that 35 minutes of cardio exercise, like running, high-speed gym workouts, calisthenics or swimming is all it takes.

I'd like to say I started with 35 minutes but it took years to get there.

As Dr. John Ratey tells us in his book *Spark: The Revolutionary New Science of Exercise and the Brain*, fitness improves all of the brain's functions, especially the learning process.

The Learning Process

Spark includes insights from a number of respected authorities, but he's the first author to use their findings to *prove* this home truth:

[The brain] is an adaptable organ that can be molded by input in much the same way a muscle can be sculpted by lifting barbells.

Ratey taught me that exercise increases the flow of brain-derived neurotrophic factor (BNDF), a chemical he calls Miracle-Gro for the brain. The most encouraging part of his findings is that you don't have to be a great athlete to pull this off.

If you're like most people, you think athletic training is tedious. But you should never put exercise in your boring file. It pays so many dividends that you're much better off learning to love it. A little goes a long way.

A recent Japanese study found that 30 minutes of jogging every other day improved the brain's executive function (planning, initiating action and predicting future events). As Ratey would say, all you have to do is lace up your running shoes.

Thirty-Five Minutes

As soon as I was able to work my way from five to 35 minutes, it didn't take long to realize that Ratey knew his stuff. Many other experts agree that 35 minutes is exactly the right amount of time for an aerobic session, road, pool or gym. Not long enough to be exhausting, not too short to be ineffective. Pretty soon I became the "35-Minute Man."

I figured it was better to spend every second of that 35 minutes going for it than wasting hours drifting through a lengthy game or some tired, old fitness routine.

So what was the best way to spend that time?

Mantras have always helped. However, when I tried to come up with an inspiring one for this program, I was stuck with the old clichés until a new one hit me.

Three steps to three miles.

That mantra has not only been true, it's inspired me to run faster and further and made me proud of my painfully slow progress.

Over time, I found that hill repeats and sprints have worked better than long, steady distance. The conditioning was a lot more concentrated, like weight lifting. For me, 35 minutes of intense working out seems like more than enough.

Visualization

Try this. Close your eyes and imagine doing the athletic feats you've always fantasized about. Maybe it's cruising over a seven-foot high-jump bar, doing an end-zone dance after a touchdown or breaking the tape at the end of a marathon. Maybe it's leaning over so an Olympic judge can slip a red, white and blue ribbon over your head. Or maybe it's a thunderous crowd cheering your name when you've won a gold medal.

With those images in mind, you can get more real by doing some coordination drills like playing catch with an irregularly shaped Reaction Ball, training with a big round Stability Ball, jumping around a Dot Drill Mat, running through a Go Ladder or threading your way through a course of Flat Agility Rings. These can be bought on the Perform Better or Power system's websites for a few bucks or you can make your own.

If these athletic routines don't feel right, maybe you need something that's more relevant to your life. It could be striding up to a podium without a limp, playing the piano for a large crowd, demonstrating a tricky new device or carrying a heavy trophy off stage. The more you visualize, the more your brain gets rewired and the more your body will reinforce those new pathways.

Improved Focus

As soon as your coordination improves, it makes sense to start working on focus. Focusing simply means forgetting about extraneous details so you can concentrate on the job at hand.

You can improve your focusing skills by throwing rocks at tin cans or aiming and shooting simple water guns. Target practice with a bow and arrow works or just plinking with an air rifle. Believe it or not, all of these take hard work and need as much concentration as firing live ammunition.

Constraint-Induced Movement Therapy

As we discussed earlier, having a TBI means your brain is sending fewer and weaker signals to the rest of your body. That means your strength isn't what it used to be and neither is your concentration. Your coordination is too often compromised by attacks of dizziness, which make everything you do a lot more work.

Experiments that deal with this problem are underway in various parts of the country. One helpful program that's being tested at the University of Alabama is called Constraint-Induced Movement Therapy, or CI therapy. This program helps restore function in the arms and legs, functioning that has been left immobile by a stroke or a brain injury.

Constraint-Induced Movement Therapy is exactly what it sounds like—it attacks the problem by restraining the movement on the unaffected side. The okay limb is tied to the patient's side so he has to use the damaged limb to do everything.

The improvements have been dramatic, and the important take-away here is that damaged nerve signals regenerate when normal ones are held against their will.

If this sounds good to you, you can do it yourself. But meanwhile, do you have to watch out for fast moves, bending, rising, running, flipping, biking and running? We'll see about that.

Since insecurity can come from mental and physical limitations, the above drills will bring back your self-confidence by increasing your abilities and killing that stubborn embarrassment.

Personally, I'm no longer too embarrassed to say I did them because they worked for me.

Left-Hand Day

I was so inspired by the restraint idea, I started doing what I called left-hand day. And pal, left hand day is no fun, but it's so effective that I'm proud to recommend it.

Since our brains are hard-wired to use the dominant hand, restraining it and forcing ourselves to do everything with our less dominant hand is much harder because it's counter-intuitive. One more time: *forcing ourselves to do everything with our less dominant hand will help our brains create new neural pathways.* The same goes for our dominant and less dominant legs, too.

This takes some getting used to, so you'll be more successful if you start with an hour and work yourself up to a whole right-handed or left-handed day. At first you'll have to do this drill consciously, but over time your brain will get more and more used to it. Before you know it, you'll even feel ambidextrous.

Hand Speed Drills

Here's a drill I seem to have invented myself.

Hold a tissue in your dominant hand and let it drop. It will waver around and take a completely unpredictable path as it flutters to the ground. Watch it drop as long as possible, then snatch it with your injured hand before it lands.

As my karate sensei used to say, "Let your right hand be your teacher and your left hand be your student."

With Min Pai's words in mind, reverse hands so your less-dominant hand can copy the normal one.

This drill reinforces the body-mind connection, making the brain work harder and faster. You'll be amazed at how quickly the affected hand gets at the snatch and grab.

Play Day

There are no movements that don't use the body and mind together, but it never hurts to reinforce the connection.

Several years before Constraint-Induced Movement Therapy was developed, Mary and I tried to re-activate my left arm by having some catches with Leo's baseball mitt, our lacrosse sticks or just a rubber ball. These were double efforts because I had to concentrate and make coordinated moves at the same time. Play days are important because they do a lot more than keep you fit—they strengthen the body-mind connection.

Sit Down

There's a good reason why you feel more organized sitting down than standing up—that's because you *are* more organized. Sitting only requires a fraction of the brain signals it takes to stand up. This leaves more of the brain free to deal with life.

Naturally, there are times when you really need to sit down and think things over. Just don't need to sit there too long.

Play Games

As I said earlier, playing games is an inefficient way to get fit, but you'll be happy to hear they have a few redeeming virtues. That's because most games are full of sudden surprises. Constantly reacting to these surprises is excellent brainwork because it forces the body to keep ad-libbing.

Games also call for fluid, curving motions that are not found in running, swimming or aerobic workouts.

Resistance Stretching

I've been stretching all my life, so you can imagine how shocked I was to learn there's a new routine that works better. Turns out I've had the wrong mental picture for years, one that called for elongating stiff muscles.

If this sounds familiar, you should know that the new method that uses *contraction* is far more effective than *elongation*. The latest stretching programs reinforce the body-mind connection by using what is called resistance stretching.

Olympic swimmer Dara Torres founded an organization whose pamphlet and DVD actually convinces athletes that *contracting and releasing a muscle* is better for its recuperation than trying to elongate it. One simply pushes or pulls a muscle in one direction while resisting that motion for about 30 seconds. When it finally releases, there's noticeably more extension.

When it comes to resistance stretching, your mind is telling your body to do the exact opposite of what you've been told all your life. But if you do it, your recovery will be much faster.

H_2O

Besides the increased sweat your new exercise routines create, you're probably taking daily medication, so it pays to drink a lot more water.

Protein

Since the brain performs well on high protein, you need 10 to 15 mg doses of it spaced out throughout the entire day. Weightlifter-type protein bars, shakes and drinks work well for this.

Eat Light

It pays to eat often and light, instead of three big squares that take a lot of energy to digest.

Look Good

Grooming and appearance are key parts of staying fit. Looking good actually helps you perform better and remember—vanity builds confidence.

The drills in this chapter have cut years off my recovery time. I had to learn them the hard way, but there's no reason why you should get heartburn, too. As we saw earlier, minimum cognitive therapy and the right drugs helped a lot, but the biggest joy is the confidence I've gotten from staying fit.

Chapter 21
New Confidence

It's hard to believe there's anything positive about a having brain injury, even if the old cliché promises a silver lining.

In my case, the silver lining has been a lot more self-confidence, the kind that people spend their whole lives trying to develop. The kind of self-confidence that either comes from years of psychological, religious and motivational programs—or it doesn't.

For me, improved confidence came from 22 years of involuntary trial and error. Twenty years that left me with dozens of new abilities, attitudes and skills. Abilities, attitudes and skills that only come from ugly experience and tiresome repetition, starving you of available energy.

Less Fatigue
I used to think of my energy supply as a giant oil lake I could always tap into. Living with a TBI has taught me otherwise. I've learned that my energy supply is a very finite commodity, a fixed amount per day instead of a boundless well of liquid gold I could afford to waste. The past 22 years have taught me that if I spent my energy unwisely, I wouldn't make it from one gusher to the next.

These days, fatigue comes on so fast that other people can see my eyes are glazing over before I stop talking and start staring into space.

But this is good news.

These shortcomings have actually made me better at directing and conserving my tiny energy supply. I've learned that any serious effort requires serious rest. I've learned that if I'm going to spend some of this valuable energy, I have to save it up. And, because I've gotten smart enough to stockpile that energy, I have some left while other people have squandered theirs. I've not only become a more careful energy-saver, I've become a more careful energy-spender.

Less Anger

Having a TBI makes me deal with more angry outbursts than the average Joe, like losing my temper over something as unimportant as a spilled drink. Luckily, anger is a motivating emotion that helps me overcome obstacles.

I remember having so many of these awful moments that one day Mary said she couldn't take it anymore and would move out if they didn't stop.

That gut-punch shocked me into taking responsibility for my actions. It gave me a reason to recognize the early signals of an outburst. And it helped me learn to head it off. Learning these feelings beforehand meant I could disappear until I thought things over.

As identifying these signs became easier, I've been able to stop my angry outbursts most of the time and life is much more balanced. But back then I couldn't see disaster coming and it almost cost me my marriage.

If you haven't got a handle on your anger, you should start paying attention to the warning signs so you can be ready for it. Over time, you'll become so good at avoiding ugly surprises they won't even happen in the first place.

If this sounds too time-consuming, be patient. Time will teach you, too.

Less Confusion

Confusion, like anger, is always lurking out there. And because it happens so many times a day, you'll get a lot of practice handling it. You'll learn that getting upset about being confused takes more time. You'll learn to unravel life's Gordian knots instead of making them tighter. You'll even learn to dump your embarrassment.

Less confusion leads to greater calm, which leads to less confusion. You'll get so used to handling it that you'll become a clearer thinker.

I was confused for such a long time so that I began to accept it as a permanent condition. For years, returning to normal was my only goal. I finally decided a pre-emptive strike was better than waiting for my symptoms to attack, and began to see my symptoms as an enemy I had to defeat. I finally got used to charging uphill through the hails of incoming fire.

This pugilistic attitude has helped me feel stronger. My natural aggressiveness along with actual physical improvement helped restore my self-confidence and made me feel like I'm back in charge.

How'd that happen? I could say things like having talk-therapy sessions right after the crash, accepting a reduced social life, hearing some friendly advice or 22 years of experience. But what really did it for me was pursuing my life-long passion—writing.

Becoming a serious writer has been the cornerstone of rebuilding my self-confidence. So much so that writing well in the morning has always set a positive tone for the whole day. I began to think of myself as a writer instead of someone who just did some writing.

Becoming a serious writer has turned a big negative into an even bigger positive. It's been a booster shot for my self-confidence if there ever was one.

More Control and Self-Control

Control and self-control are not the same thing. Think about it— there's a big difference between behaving yourself and dealing with your environment.

What happens in your environment is *not* up to you. It's unpredictable, spontaneous and totally surprising. Anything can happen and it usually does. However, as we discussed in earlier chapters, minimum control is possible and you can get better at recognizing the early danger signs.

On the other hand, losing your temper is completely up to you. If you don't keep it in check, you'll be doing things you'll regret forever. This one is simple, pal. Just take a deep breath and *don't do it*. If you do, you'll pay the price.

Everybody loses confidence when they lose control, and they won't feel better until they get it back. When you have a brain injury, regaining control doesn't just feel better—it's vital. And having a new kind of self-confidence will mean you'll never have to settle for normal again (whatever that is).

Your new self confidence means it will not only be easier to say goodbye to the old you, it will be easier to say hello to the better you. A more relaxed you. A more independent you. A prouder you.

Soon you'll be proud of not assuming anything. Proud of not taking anything for granted. Proud of looking forward to the years ahead. Proud to know you're on the right road. Proud that your insecurities are on the run. Proud to believe that the new you is still you.

So since your TBI symptoms have become sources of strength, does that mean having a brain injury is a good thing? No way, but it does mean your very limitations can make you stronger. So strong you'll be eager to accept responsibility for yourself and be proactive again.

It's much easier to talk about than do, but stay with it, pal. Walking the walk will give you more self-confidence than talking the talk ever will.

Chapter 22
New Fun

Unfortunately the American idea of fun always seems to come with raucous excitement. Either the loud cheering, angry booing and aggressive jostling that we find in the new stadiums or the thumping music, smoke-filled lounges and dry-humping we find on night club dance floors.

My old list had exciting public events like live concerts and cocktail parties, as well as endurance events with a lot of spectators—10k's, triathlons, half marathons, bike races and crowded surf contests.

My new list is far less external and a lot more internal. It's not only gotten calmer, quieter and safer—it's more private, more predictable and much more controllable, not to mention less intense and a lot more doable.

Reading has become an obsession. Early-morning coffee is sacrosanct. Netflix and TiVo are my daily breaks, and learning about California wines has become a serious hobby.

Even though I miss the good old days, my definition of fun just had to change. The amount of fun I could handle in a day had to come way down. I had to stop taking myself too seriously and I needed more daily breaks, aka TBI vacations. Since I've never taken an unforced TBI vacation, the ill effects of exhaustion still surprise me as if they've never happened before.

My anxiety attacks don't go away in a minute—they last long enough to throw a whole day out of whack. I've had to make sure my pals know I'm happier with less fun and to not to push me to the breaking point. Some friends never want to go home, but I finally learned how to kick them out nicely and think of fun in a new way. Think about it like this:

Less fun is more fun and more fun is less fun.

Commotion, shoving and confusion are the last thing you should have to endure when you have a brain injury.

So don't.

There's no way fun should be defined by anyone else, least of all those gorgeous models in those glossy ad campaigns. Or those laughing families in the expensive TV commercials and slick catalogue. And especially not those fast-talking television announcers who shill those hot new computer games.

No, you need a new definition of fun, one that has nothing to do with pop culture. You need a new definition that's yours and yours alone.

Everybody has their own idea of fun and mine is probably not yours. But once I started thinking about it, it wasn't long before I realized that my new list had to be completely different from my old list.

Different fun, sure. Less fun, okay. But no fun? No way. I've reached a point where I can have fun laughing at my own TBI symptoms. Spoofing my physical and mental limitations has gotten to be a new source of jokes.

Like laughing at my own clumsiness and telling Mary that I fell down when I just tripped for a second. Or cracking up about my illegible handwriting on our shopping list. One day, Mary thought

I wrote "define those oracles" when I really wrote "mandarin oranges." Then, there's talking seriously about not needing a shower today, calling convenience food today's real gourmet cooking, and how I'm too old to understand how to work a computer.

But wait, there's more. I also joke about my short-term memory loss, like swearing I've never seen a movie I just saw last week (I call myself the demented husband). I ask Mary if she can still recognize me with my new sun tan. There's sarcasm about getting lost in our apartment or needing an instruction manual to shave. But the silliest thing happens when I stand up to leave a restaurant and get dizzy on the way out. Mary and I are sure all the other couples are shaking their heads and whispering, "Look, Marge. I don't think that guy should have ordered that second bottle of wine."

Remember when I said that I originally created www.philslott.com in the hopes it would be seen by the right literary agent? When no one even noticed it, I kept it going because I thought it was such a kick.

My website content is entitled *What's the Big Idea?* The Big Idea section includes permanent excerpts from my unpublished novels, short stories and essays as well as three segments that I change weekly: Thought du Jour (TDJ), Weird Facts and Obscure Quotes.

Thought du Jour is a contrarian list of outrageous observations, ironic thoughts, personal conclusions, politically incorrect opinions and daily musings. The past TDJ's always stay listed, but here's a tiny sample of the more current ones.

Everything in life is a half hour too long.
Idea thieves deserve the death penalty.
What this world needs is more sax.
Why Velcro when you can Teflon?
If you're not the boss, you have to work for some other asshole who is.
Pollination is plant boffing.

Obscure Quotes is a collection of well-written sayings by others as well as thoughts that come from movies, TV news, magazine articles, friends and family members.

"If you're not busy being born, you're busy dying."
BOB DYLAN

"If you don't cry and have an orgasm after you've ridden a good Icelandic horse, you've missed out."
DAN SLOTT

"If one cop knocks on the door, it's a conversation. If two cops knock on the door it's a raid."
COP IN "THE MERRY GENTLEMEN"

"Procrastinate now—don't put it off."
ELLEN DEGENERES

"You have atomic bombs, and we have suicide bombers."
TALIBAN FIGHTER

The Weird Facts section is just that—a collection of weird facts that come from everywhere.

25% of people over 65 years of age have lost all of their teeth.

The striped mittenfish (a deep water species, recently discovered in the Java Sea) can change its sex at will by turning its entire body inside out.

The liver is the only internal human organ capable of natural re-growing lost tissue; as little as 25% of a liver can regenerate into a whole liver.

Modern Toilet is a restaurant in Taipei with a modern décor and a full-on toilet theme. All 100 seats in the crowded diner are made from toilet bowls, not chairs. Sinks, faucets and gender-coded "WC" signs appear throughout the three-story facility. It's one of 12 in an island-wide chain of eateries.

The South China Mall in Dongguan, China has 7.1 million square feet of floor space and occupies a total land area of 9.6 million square feet. It can hold more than 2,000 stores in its southern China location in Guangdong province. It features a number of zones modeled on international cities, favorite destinations and popular regions including Paris, Rome, Venice, Egypt, Amsterdam, California and Caribbean.

John Isner of the United States outlasted Nicolas Mahut of France in the fifth set of their epic three-day match at Wimbledon. They fought for 11 hours and 5 minutes, breaking all records for length of match, games played and aces served.

Now back to less factual fun.

Not everybody's as funny as Jerry Seinfeld, but his show about nothing reminds us that everyday life can be hysterical.

When you live in Hawaii, it's almost impossible not to be sarcastic about the constant flow of tourists and the over-use of the word "aloha." Mary and I have fun with both.

Every time we see a clean white car with a Z in its plate, we know it's full of "rent-a-people."

Most visitors hope they'll be taken as locals if they just keep saying, "Aloha!" The ones who keep saying, "Mahalo!" are sure they're already locals.

We also crack up mimicking local MC's who always greet their audiences with "AHH-LOOOOO-HAH!" so we answer our phone with "HELLO—HAH!"

We have an on-going worst-word contest. Right now, Mary's is *detritus* and mine is *renal.*

We often giggle about changing people's names to fit their behavior. Like when the hotel's lap pool was stuck with an older guy who sunbathed nude every morning at seven. Mary and I started calling him Too-Tan-Man. After that, it wasn't long until the manager told Too-Tan-Man that nudity was inappropriate anywhere on the resort grounds.

None of these is as good as a Seinfeld joke, but hey, he's a pro.

If you think having a TBI means the end of fun, think again. The list goes on and on.

From writing silly song lyrics to memory games of all kinds. From telling about early childhood pranks to reading funny authors like Tom Wolfe, Robert Crais and Donald Westlake. From acting out movie scenes in old movies to e-mail relationships with funny friends. Ordering the right stuff online is fun. Even remembering the copy from early TV and radio commercials can be a hoot. "Veg-a-matic: slices, dices, even crushes ice. Look at those slices—perfect every time!"

However, two things that most people think of as fun should probably be avoided: sudden noises like firecrackers and wild rides at amusement parks. Any sudden BANG! will shock you into a reaction that's upsetting because it's involuntary. Skip those crazy rides at amusement parks. The repeated shifts of balance you'll experience on rides like The Intimidator, bumper cars or the parachute jump will bring on big bouts of nauseous vertigo.

No firecrackers—no problem. No Tilt-a-Whirl—no problem. But no surfing?

Hmmmmmm...

I'd like to say that if I took my board out to the breaks every morning for weeks, if I was willing to wipe out and climb back on for days or watch hundreds of unridden waves go by, maybe, just maybe, I'd be able to stand up and ride a one-footer. But that's a hell of a lot of work for a maybe, don't you think? I feel like I've lost too much time as it is and I don't want to waste another second.

At this point, it's just better to accept the truth and move on. Here goes:

The truth is, I have so much vertigo I get dizzy just riding up and down on the bumps in a small bay. The truth is, I no longer paddle fast enough to catch a swell or stay in front of the white water. The truth is, I can no longer handle wipeouts or being held under. The truth is, it's so gnarly out there and I've lost so much control that I'm afraid to surf. After all, lack of control leads straight to fear, right? And that's no fun.

These days, I'm having fun entertaining readers by telling them stories and making new points by writing essays. I hope my essays tell people something they've never thought of before. I hope my fiction entertains them with tales they've never read before. Writing makes me feel like a magician who can state a meaningful truth in a few words.

Less fun is more fun and more fun is less fun.

Chapter 23
The New Normal

Mary

"Phi-hil, I thought it was your turn to empty the trash!"

"We were supposed to meet at the gym."

"I have no idea where your keys are."

The day finally arrived when I stopped expecting disaster at every turn. It was as if I suddenly woke up and discovered that I no longer had to hold my breath when Phil was doing chores in the kitchen. I became more concerned about arriving on time than being hit by another drunk driver. I stopped waking up each time Phil's breathing seemed to stop.

Anxiety slipped away like the morning mist. One day I was raw and jumpy about the big, bad world and the next day I was worried about having a good movie to watch.

It occurred to me that life is never the same from day to day. Crashes happen. People die. Children are born. Careers change. Families move and limitations are always holding somebody back.

The world is shifting around us all the time and we are changing, too. The way we think and what we do. Our ambitions and desires are always evolving.

All of the focus on Phil being who he used to be reminded me that I'm not who I used to be either. To paraphrase the lyrics of a country song: *I used to be somebody, but now I am somebody else.*

How could either of us be the same people after such a life-changing event? We couldn't and we aren't. We're back to normal again, but we're somebody else.

Before the accident I never knew how wonderful "regular" could be. The mundane became joyous. Normality became a luxury. Waking up without that ugly wave of dread became sweet time. Now Phil and I sit in our chairs with cups of coffee, read the news, write up the day's schedule or chat about the BBC's newest headlines on badger culls and hedgehog crises.

Phil's recovery process has been like losing my backache. I used to wake up with painful aches day after day and pray the pain would disappear. When the day arrived that the pain was gone, I didn't remember that it ever hurt.

The yearning for the way it was, thoughts about how Phil used to be and the endless quest for the past, have all passed. We are finally living in the present and enjoying life the way it is, *right now!* I've quit comparing the old Phil to the new Phil. And I'm overjoyed that he is right across the table telling funny stories from his Greenwich Village days, complaining about politicians and regaling me with stories of his schnauzer Fuzzy. He holds my hand when I've had a hard day.

Accepting the new Phil has meant we have stopped talking about what used to happen and started focusing on making new things happen, on making a different life that works for both of us.

What is life like now? During the darkest days after the crash, I learned to paint. I am now an official artist! I paint every day when I'm not preparing for shows or working with galleries. I spend a fair amount of time in my studio, away from the quiet hub of the house. It's a whole new world for me with new friends and associates.

Phil writes every day and works out at the gym. He reads and keeps up on the world news. At the end of our days, we have a glass of wine with dinner and compare stories.

It's a smaller life but a sweet one.

We have rediscovered the faith that the days will continue and that our love will carry us through.

Life is good.

Chapter 24
Better Days

The worst is over and the bad old days are finally ebbing away. How the hell do I keep them from coming back and haunting me again?

It seems to me the best way to do that is by sticking to a regular daily schedule. A regular schedule is like having dependable footing when I run. A safe place that has the feelings I only get in my own neighborhood. A warm place that delivers the comfort of my favorite chair. A dependable place that makes me feel secure, because I know it's always there.

Since stress demands so much energy, having a regular schedule has cut the surprises in life and given me a lot more go-power. A regular schedule may be comforting, but if I want to accomplish anything important, it has to be the *right* schedule as well.

For starters, it's always paid to do the most important things in the morning when I have more energy and the most positive attitude. The morning is when I really feel like attacking work, doing hard chores or anything else I'm committed to.

If you're a workaholic, so be it. But if your job is just about a paycheck, you'll be better off with a demanding avocation. Try to choose one with prepossessing daily tasks and built-in goals, one that has challenges to overcome and victories to celebrate. Challenges like becoming an expert at your hobby, winning races or pursuing your passion. Challenges like being a dependable caregiver for someone else.

I think of myself as living from mini-victory to mini-victory. And if today was a great day, I never forget to write GREAT DAY! in my calendar.

Sticking to the right schedule may be the best way to keep those bad old days from coming back. But, you also have to accept some needta's, haveta's, oughta's, gotta's, shoulda's, betta's and might-as-well's.

You needta get used to the feeling that you've been there and done that. You haveta get used to taking drugs every day of your life. You oughta realize that all social encounters cost the same amount of energy. After all, it takes the same number of ergs to be with a close friend as it does to be with some asshole.

You gotta get used to reminders that go beyond written lists to spoken lists, like telling yourself out loud to have a carbo-energizer before the gym and a protein bar to help you recover.

You betta avoid upsets early in the day. Otherwise, they'll snowball and you'll find out you shoulda.

You needta take frequent breaks since you know it's good to keep busy. It's a double if you use your daily chores as breaks.

And you might as well do a lot of might-as-well's.

Weekly schedules work, too. It's comforting to know that certain weekdays call for writing sessions in the morning and gym workouts in the afternoon. Or that Sunday is a day off and all you're going to do is sit in the sun, read, or watch the bad news shows on TV.

It's great when those needta's haveta's, oughta's, gotta's, shoulda's, betta's and might-as-well's become wanna's. Things you wanna do because they make you feel good.

It's taken over 6,000 daily schedules for my better days to sneak up on me, sort of like paddling out of some rocky rapids and into a smooth, wide river.

Whew—6,000 days to reach a balance between too much and not enough! Six thousand days to learn that two tough events a day are one too many. Six thousand days to learn that even small talk is hard work. Six thousand days to learn that one social occasion a week is more than enough. Six thousand days to have fun again. Six thousand days to be happy with less.

But now that less is more, I'm sleeping better, enjoying the gym, having more fun in the sun and I'm relaxed about my daily routine because I always know what's next.

I haven't had this many good days in years.

You're not going to wake up one day to find that everything's absolutely perfect. Your better days will sneak up slowly until one day you find that you've got more energy, you're a clearer thinker and, amazing as it seems, you've got a cooler head.

Unfortunately, this takes years.

Years to accept your new limitations as facts of life. Years to make dealing with them routine. Years to get used to being on a regular daily schedule. Years before you can think of boredom as a luxury. Years to get used to living in a smaller universe. Years before you can regain control of life. Years to restore your self-confidence. Years to go from saying "I'm lucky to be alive," to thinking "My best days are yet to come." And years to realize that it takes years to get to your better days.

You may have already gotten some glimmers of these better days. If so, you should know those tiny glimmers are just previews of the show that's yet to come.

By the time the curtains open again, the house lights will be on and your mini-victories will be so commonplace that they'll become expectations. You'll have such a positive attitude that half empty will become half full, partly cloudy will become partly sunny, overcooked will be a nice try, burnt will be crispy and you'll be happy about gale-force winds because they'll blow the pollution away.

Dumping depression has helped me in too many ways to count. Working on sequencing has made me more organized. Dealing with anxiety has made me calmer. Dealing with vertigo has given me much better balance.

I've become way better at handling obstacles in general. Positivism has armed me against negativism. I feel like a proud aggressor instead of an embarrassed victim. Good has become good enough, and I'm even asking how good do things really have to be?

Maybe it's hard to admit, but if your life has really gotten better—great! And if "better days" sounds like the title of a bad soap opera, so be it. Meanwhile, as us New York Mets fans used to say, you gotta believe.

Chapter 25
If...

If you can dream—and not make dreams your master;
If you can think—and not make thoughts your aim;
If you can meet with Triumph and Disaster
And treat those two impostors just the same;
If you can bear to hear the truth you've spoken
Twisted by knaves to make a trap for fools,
Or watch the things you gave your life to, broken,
And stoop and build 'em up with worn-out tools:

If you can make one heap of all your winnings
And risk it on one turn of pitch-and-toss,
And lose, and start again at your beginnings
And never breathe a word about your loss;
If you can force your heart and nerve and sinew
To serve your turn long after they are gone,
And so hold on when there is nothing in you
Except the Will which says to them: 'Hold on!'

If you can talk with crowds and keep your virtue,
Or walk with Kings—nor lose the common touch,

If neither foes nor loving friends can hurt you,
If all men count with you, but none too much;
If you can fill the unforgiving minute
With sixty seconds' worth of distance run,
Yours is the Earth and everything that's in it,
And—which is more—you'll be a Man, my son!
"IF" BY RUDYARD KIPLING

Kipling's poem, *If*, meant a lot to the brave soldiers of the 19th century, but you're a brave soldier, too. And since accepting some new truths will help you win the most important fight of your life, we should wind down by reviewing these ifs, too.

If you can stick to a regular schedule…
If you can relax about taking drugs every day…
If you can handle social embarrassment…
If you can get used to constant reminders…
If you can avoid getting upset in the morning…
If you can take frequent breaks…
If you can handle short-term memory losses…
If you can stand frequent bouts of fatigue…
If you can keep from blowing your cool…
If you can stop being a crazed perfectionist…
If you can be happy with a slow recovery…

Nobody wants a life that's full of scheduling snafus, drug paranoia, social embarrassment, constant reminders, early upsets, over-working, forgotten occasions, total exhaustion, anxiety or compulsiveness. Nobody wants a stalled recovery. I'm sure you'll have this all under control one day, and keeping those bad old days from coming back will be a forgotten goal.

Remember that better days take as much getting used to as those bad old days ever did. If you can accept that good simply isn't good enough and if you can get used to all the needta's, haveta's, oughta's, gotta's, shoulda's, betta's and might-as-well's that have been driving you crazy, you'll sleep better, worry less and make fewer boo-hoo's.

If this seems like going to grammar school, so be it. As our teachers used to say, if you memorize Kipling's last *if,* you won't be sorry.

> *If you can fill the unforgiving minute*
> *With sixty seconds' worth of distance run,*
> *Yours is the Earth and everything that's in it,*
> *And—which is more—you'll be a Man my son!*

Chapter 26
The Brand-New You

You can make it if you try.
ROLLING STONES

There was no such thing as a full recovery until I passed hundreds of challenging "if tests," but somehow I did. The last thing I need right now is another funeral for what's been lost. No way! It's time to celebrate what's been found. It's time to skip the lost department and go straight to the found department.

I know it's hard to believe that having serious limitations has actually made me a better person, but it has. Living with a brain injury has been like living without several key senses. And just like the people who lose their eyesight and find their other senses get stronger to compensate for it, mine did, too.

My sister-in-law, Nancy, is a living example of this. Nancy is nearly blind. And, even though more than 90 percent of her vision is gone, you'd never know it. Her other senses have not only filled in by getting more acute, she's developed an amazing memory. She's gotten so fast at memorizing new house layouts and negotiating her way around them, in 15 minutes you'd think she was home.

Nancy admits this is hard work and she doesn't do it unless she has to. But over time she's developed the willpower to deal with it. She not only insists on being independent, she maintains the positive attitude that makes it possible.

She is always saying things like, "I know where I am," and "Don't worry, I know where the curbs are."

Of course, Nancy does get lost on occasion, and she's tripped on those curbs more than once.

Bad news? No way!

I'd like to say Nancy did all this by trying, but trying is too weak a word. Trying assumes the possibility of failure and is a kind of built-in apology for an unsuccessful attempt:

Well, at least she tried.

Bullshit. Nancy has attacked her problems head on and taught me that I should, too. Remember: attacking is the booster shot that has always gotten me from one mini-victory to the next.

Nancy's a great example of how any obstacle can be overcome, how attack works better than retreat, how limitations are just challenges and how beating her disability works like a secret map.

A secret map?

Yes. The same map that has helped me find the most valuable treasures of all. Treasures like increased focus, intensity, drive and willpower. Treasures like more independence. Treasures that have helped me stand up to constant repetition. Treasures that have helped me make complex movements. Treasures that have improved my learning process by connecting it to exercise. Treasures like more self-confidence. Solid gold treasures that are as good as drugs when it comes to fighting off depression and anxiety.

These guys make the point much better than I can:

"If you can't, you must. If you must, you can."
ANTHONY ROBBINS

"Man often becomes what he believes himself to be. If I keep on saying to myself that I cannot do a certain thing, it is possible that I may end by really becoming incapable of doing it. On the contrary, if I have the belief that I can do it, I shall surely acquire the capacity to do it even if I may not have it at the beginning."
MAHATMA GANDHI

*You can't always get what you want
But if you try sometimes you just might find
You get what you need.*
ROLLING STONES

"If you change the way you look at things, the things you look at change."
DR. WAYNE DYER

"If we always do what we've always done, we will get what we've always got."
ADAM URBANSKI

"If you can imagine it you can achieve it. If you can dream it, you can become it."
WILLIAM ARTHUR WARD

It won't be long until your mini-victories make your hard side harder by making concentration easier, by making your focus sharper by making your reactions faster by helping you get it right the first time, by helping you think before you act and by making you braver. It's only a matter of time until those mini-victories ensure that you are slaloming through the flagpoles of life.

Defeating your enemy will make your soft side softer, too. You'll have a new understanding of adversity. You'll have a deeper appreciation of caring, you'll become more forgiving, more sympathetic and a lot more empathetic.

If.

ACKNOWLEDGMENTS

It is impossible to mention every person who helped out during my recovery. My family, friends and the medical personnel who saved my life and got me through the long days of confusion deserve special attention. After all, they made this book possible.

Hunter Armstrong   Judith Aston
Darien Gee   Linda & Nate Goldstein
Shannon Heringer   Dr. Mary Hibbard
Rogene Huber-Berejana   Ian Mattoch
Elizabeth Morgan   Kevin Quirk
Wendy Rundel   Sylvia Sepielli
Amory Slott   Dan & Molly Slott
Nancy Spears   Ron & Mary Spears

And thanks to Matthew Pearce at Waimea Instant Printing for the cover design.

Made in the USA
Charleston, SC
23 March 2015